MW00642184

DESIDERIUS ERASMUS OF ROTTERDAM

ON COPIA OF
WORDS AND IDEAS

(De Utraque Verborum ac Rerum Copia)

MEDIÆVAL PHILOSOPHICAL TEXTS IN TRANSLATION

No. 12

MARQUETTE UNIVERSITY PRESS

MILWAUKEE WISCONSIN 2007

DESIDERIUS ERASMUS OF ROTTERDAM

ON COPIA OF
WORDS AND IDEAS

(*De Utraque Verborum ac Rerum Copia*)
Translated from the Latin
With an Introduction

by

DONALD B. KING
Professor of English

College of Mt. St. Joseph On-the-Ohio

AND

H. DAVID RIX
Formerly Professor of English

Pennsylvania State University

FIFTH PRINTING

MARQUETTE UNIVERSITY PRESS
MILWAUKEE, WISCONSIN 2007

Library of Congress Catalogue Number: 63-10892

© 1963, 1999, 2005 The Marquette University Press
Milwaukee, Wisconsin

ISBN-10: 0-87462-212-3
ISBN-13: 978-087462-212-6
Printed in the United States of America

Second Printing 1982
Third Printing 1999
Fourth Printing 2005
Fifth Printing 2007

MARQUETTE UNIVERSITY PRESS
MILWAUKEE

The Association of Jesuit University Presses

CONTENTS

Translator's Introduction 1

Note to the Reader 9

BOOK I

CHAPTER I   *That the Aspiration to Copia Is Dangerous* 11

CHAPTER II   *By Whom Copia Was Developed and by Whom Practiced* 12

CHAPTER III   *How Authors Have Indulged in a Display of Copia* 13

CHAPTER IV   *To Whom Unrestrained Copia Has Been Attributed as a Fault* 14

CHAPTER V   *That It Is Characteristic of the Same Artist to Speak Both Concisely and Copiously* 14

CHAPTER VI   *Concerning Those Who Strive for Either Conciseness or Copia Foolishly* 15

CHAPTER VII   *That Copia Is Twofold* 15

CHAPTER VIII   *For What Things This Training Is Useful* 16

CHAPTER IX   *By What Methods of Training This Faculty May Be Developed* 17

CHAPTER X   *First Precept Concerning Copia* 18

CHAPTER XI   *The First Method of Varying by* Synonymia 19

CHAPTER XII   *The Words Peculiar to Different Ages* 24

CHAPTER XIII   *Method of Varying by* Enallage *or* Ἑτέρωσις 25

CHAPTER XIV   *Method of Varying by* Antonomasia 27

CHAPTER XV   *Method of Varying by* Periphrasis 27

CHAPTER XVI   *Method of Varying by* Metaphor 28

CHAPTER XVII   *Reciprocal Metaphors* 29

CHAPTER XVIII   *Method of Varying by* Allegory 30

CHAPTER XIX   *Method of Varying by* Catachresis 30

CHAPTER XX   *Variation by Onomatopoeia* 31

CHAPTER XXI   *Method of Varying by* Metalepsis.................... 31

CHAPTER XXII   *Method of Varying by* Metonymy 32

CHAPTER XXIII   *Method of Varying by* Synecdoche 33

CHAPTER XXIV   *Method of Varying by* Aequipollentia 33

CHAPTER XXV   *Method of Varying by* Comparatives 34

CHAPTER XXVI   *Method of Varying by Change of Relatives*.............. 34

CHAPTER XXVII   *Method of Varying by Amplification*.................. 35

CHAPTER XXVIII   *Method of Varying by* Hyperbole 35

CHAPTER XXIX   *Method of Varying by* Μείωσις, *i.e.,* Diminutio 35

CHAPTER XXX   *Method of Varying by* Compositio 36

CHAPTER XXXI   *Method of Varying through* Σύνταξις, *i.e.,* Constructio.... 37

CHAPTER XXXII   *Method of Varying through Changing the Figure in*
                 Various Ways 37

CHAPTER XXXIII   *Practice* 38

BOOK II

First Method of Embellishing 43

Second Method of Varying 46

Third Method 46

Fourth Method 47

Fifth Method 47

Egressio, Sixth Method of Amplifying 55

Seventh Method 56

Eighth Method 57

Ninth Method of Enlarging 58

Tenth Method of Amplifying 60

Eleventh Method 66

On the Multiplication of the Parts of a Speech 97

Epilogue 104

Peroration 106

Translator's Introduction

I. THE WORKS OF ERASMUS

On a trip to England in the summer of 1499 Erasmus met several men who were to become lifelong friends, Thomas More, John Colet, and others enthusiastic about classical literature. Particularly fruitful was his encounter with Colet, who enkindled in Erasmus what was to become a major ambition: to revivify the theology of the schools with a deeper study of Holy Scripture in the original languages and also of the works of the early Church Fathers. With this aspect of his work we are not here directly concerned. Suffice it to say that after years of preparation and after he had become the most sought after scholar in Europe he finally published in 1516 his Latin version of the New Testament together with a Greek text. The same year saw his edition of the works of St. Jerome. From then until his death twenty years later there came from his pen revised forms of his New Testament, paraphrases of large parts of Scripture, and numerous editions of the works of the Fathers of the Church. None of this work is now of serious value textually, but in its time it constituted a tremendous exploitation of the recently discovered printer's art in what Erasmus hoped would be a renaissance of Christian faith and practice springing from a return to the sources.

Upon returning to Paris from England in 1500 Erasmus published the work which more than any other was to serve as the basis for his literary reputation. This was the *Adagia*, a collection of about 800 Latin proverbs (later much enlarged) with appropriate comments by Erasmus. The *Adagia* may be said to typify Erasmus' other major ambition: to replace medieval learning with the riches of Greek and Latin letters, or as it was then called, the New Learning. Other writings of Erasmus intended to open up to his contemporaries the riches of classical style and matter include the *De copia*, its companion volume, the *De conscribendis epistolis*, and the extremely popular and witty dialogues of the *Colloquia*. As a measure of his indefatigable industry it may be recalled that the first collected edition of his works, published in 1540, four years after his death, filled twelve large folio volumes. In addition, eleven volumes were required for the publication of his correspondence by P. S. Allen and H. M. Allen in the years from 1906 to 1947.[1]

II. THE EDITIONS OF THE *De Copia*

The first edition of the *De duplici copia verborum ac rerum* of Erasmus was completed during Erasmus' third and most lengthy visit

---

[1] Erasmus, *Opus Epistolarum*, eds. P.S. Allen and H. M. Allen (Oxford: Oxford University Press, 1906-47) (hereafter cited as Allen).

to England (1509-1514). It is dedicated appropriately to John Colet for use in St. Paul's School, which he had recently opened in London. The first of many printings of the work was issued from the press of Badius at Paris on July 15, 1512 in a volume which included the *De ratione studii* and some minor writings:

> D. Erasmi Roterodami de duplici Copia rerum ac verborum commentarii duo. De ratione studii & instituendi pueros commentarii totidem. De puero Iesu Concio scholastica: & Quaedam carmina ad eamdem rem pertinentia. Venundantur in aedibus Ascensianis.[2]

After Erasmus left England in 1514, he visited Strasbourg. There he gave Matthias Schurer (who had already run off a few unauthorized printings of the work) the first revised form of the *De copia* which Schurer printed in December, 1514.[3] Later Erasmus went to Basle and gave the printer, Froben, a corrected copy of the *De copia* which appeared in print in 1517.[4] Then, in 1526 he issued another revised version of the work from the press of Froben. Driven away from Basle in 1529 by the excesses of the Reformers, he retired to Freiburg. From there he sent his third and final revision of the *De copia* to the Froben press in 1534.[5]

The present translation was made from a seventeenth century copy of the *De copia* which had first been collated with a copy of the first edition of Schurer, dated January, 1513, with a copy of the first revised edition, published by Schurer in December of 1514, with a copy of the second revised edition, published by Froben in 1526, and with a copy of the 1540 Basle *Opera Omnia* edition representing the text as it appeared in Erasmus' third and last revision. No significant differences were found between the seventeenth century copy and the Basle edition of 1540.

One indication of the success of the *De copia* is to be found in a summary of its printing history.[6] During the lifetime of Erasmus at least eighty-five editions of the *De copia* were published by a great variety of printers throughout western Europe and especially in Germany, France, and the Low Countries. After 1550 the demand for the book abated somewhat but the total number of printings during the sixteenth century was well above 150, and there were scattered editions published subsequently as late as 1824. Mention should also be

---

[2] Copy in the library of Harvard University.

[3] Allen, Ep. 311.

[4] Allen, Ep. 462.

[5] For an account of Erasmus' habits in dealing with printers, see P. S. Allen, *Erasmus* (Oxford: Oxford University Press, 1934), pp. 109-37.

[6] H. D. Rix, "The Editions of Erasmus' *De Copia*," *Studies in Philology*, XLIII (1946), 595-618.

made of such works as a catechism of questions and answers on its subject matter prepared by Lucas Lossius (1508-1582). The first of several editions of this digest appeared about 1550. Then there was the *Enchiridion ad verborum copia* of Thierry Morel with fifteen or more printings between 1525 and 1551, and the *De utraque copia verborum et rerum praecepta* of Andre des Freux, S.J., with several printings during the third quarter of the century. Erasmus' writings were very popular in Spain but difficult to obtain there; one way of providing the subject matter was to reproduce it in works of a Spanish author. This was done for the *De copia* in the *Rhetorica en lengua Castellana* (anonymous) printed in Alcala in 1541 and containing a section on copia borrowed from Erasmus. In England, where several editions of the *De copia* were published during the sixteenth century, and one as late as 1823, the *Treatise on Schemes and Tropes,* 1550, incorporated a partial summary of Book II in English.

III.   ANALYSIS OF THE *De Copia*

The general plan of the *De copia* was probably suggested to Erasmus by a passage in the tenth book of Quintilian's *Institutio oratoria.* The first chapter of that book bore the title "De copia verborum" in editions of the work printed during the lifetime of Erasmus and the phrase "copia rerum ac verborum" (echoing a similar phrase in Book III of Cicero's *De oratore*) appears early in the chapter. Quintilian eschewed any discussion of methods for attaining copia rerum on the ground that ideas (rerum) are peculiar to a given case so that a general approach is impracticable. His treatment of copia of words, moreover, is extremely brief, most of the chapter on this subject being devoted to a critical discussion of Greek and Roman poets, dramatists, historians, orators, and philosophers from the point of view of their value in the education of orators. This left a clear field for Erasmus to supply the pedagogical details omitted by his illustrious predecessor. It will be noted that there is no mention of Quintilian in the dedicatory epistle to Colet, but rather only of some minor writers, and that Erasmus claims credit for being the first to think through and develop the subject. But of course Erasmus is not the only great writer to be silent about sources.

Book I of the *De copia,* on copia of words, opens with a general discussion on the nature and value of copia. This leads to a chapter on the first precept of copia, that the writer's language should be pure, elegant, appropriate, Latin. That this chapter is not succeeded by others developing the second precept of copia, the third, etc., may be explained by the author's rather haphazard methods of organizing material. Instead there comes next (chapter 11) the first method of varying—by the use of synonyms. Here Erasmus is following Quintilian closely, even to the illustration, *ensis, gladius*. But before treating the second method of varying, Erasmus digresses at length on a topic arising from the first precept of copia, warning his readers about the use of words that are low, uncommon, poetic, and so on, through some ten categories. By far the greater part of this material on good usage appeared for the first time in the final revision of the text of 1534.

The next twenty chapters continue with methods of varying, for the key to the richness of style so highly prized in the Renaissance era was the repetition of an idea in skillfully varied diction. The particular methods that Erasmus recommends (following a suggestion of Quintilian) include the use of the traditional ten tropes—metaphor, synecdoche, etc.—and of other figures as well.

Here a few words may be said about the relation of the *De copia* to traditional rhetorical theory. In ancient times the training of the orator was discussed under five headings: (1) methods of generating cogent arguments (*inventio;* Books iv and v of the *Institutio oratoria*), (2) appropriate arrangement of material in the oration (*dispositio;* Book vi), (3) rules for cultivating an admirable style (*elocutio;* Books viii-x), (4) devices to help the orator memorize and (5) deliver his material effectively (*memoria and pronuntiatio;* Book xi). The treatise of Quintilian represents the rhetorical tradition, inherited by the Romans from the Greeks, at its best, free from both pedantry and meretricious display.

The political atmosphere of the later empire contributed to the decline of the oratorical ideals of an earlier age, and the emphasis in the teaching of rhetoric shifted to style. Furthermore, style came to be identified mainly with the use of figures of speech as ornaments. This emphasis is reflected in the text which served as the principal source transmitting rhetorical doctrine in the West through the medieval centuries to the renaissance period, the *Rhetorica ad Herennium*, long attributed to Cicero. The last of its four books, in length nearly equal to the first three combined, is devoted to style and the figures of speech receive the major attention. Erasmus borrowed material from this text for some of his illustrations.

Several different methods of classifying the figures were in vogue. Quintilian divides them into (1) tropes, the use of words in other than their normal signification and (2) figures or schemes (a) of thought and (b) of words. In the *ad Herennium* the tropes are included with the figures of words. Classifications similar to these are found in the numerous rhetorical textbooks that appeared during the sixteenth century. Erasmus himself takes no interest in these matters. In fact, he

[4]

appears to demonstrate his independence of these systems which seldom rise above the level of pedantry. For he freely interposes among the tropes a selection of figures of words and of thoughts to suit his purpose.

Following upon the last of the methods of varying words by the use of figures, Erasmus in chapter 33 gives a dazzling exhibition of their application, writing a hundred fifty variations on the sentence, "Tuae literae me magnopere delectarunt," and two hundred on "Semper dum vivam tui meminero." In this way the greatest master of copious style demonstrates to his disciples how to put principles into practice.

The remainder of Book I is essentially a thesaurus or collection of formulas arranged under a variety of headings useful to students of composition. It is the part of the *De copia* that underwent the principal expansion in successive revisions and that is of least interest today. In 1512, Book I included 153 chapters; in 1526, the number was extended to 171 and in 1534 to 206. Since only the first 33 chapters of Book I are presented in this translation, a few illustrations from the latter part are given here. Chapters 34 to 94, which run from a half dozen lines to several pages in length, exhibit methods of varying grammatical or syntactic forms. For example, chapter 46, the longest of all, is concerned with methods of varying superlative expressions, and contains extensive lists of such phrases as sweeter than honey, more hateful than death, wiser than Nestor, etc. Chapter 66 gives about twenty-five different formulas for citing an author. Chapters 94 to 206 are shorter chapters, many of them running only a few lines, and list variations on individual words or phrases somewhat in the fashion of a modern thesaurus except that the arrangement is haphazard rather than alphabetical. Thus Chapter 159 lists these formulas for varying *solitudinis*:

He lives by himself. He talks to himself. He is alone. He is solitary. He proceeds unattended. He walks alone. It is not safe to walk in deserted places, etc.

Having employed the tropes and schemes of rhetoric to develop the methods of copia for words, Erasmus turned to the topics of dialectic for the methods of copia rerum. In Book II there is very little theory and a great deal of illustration. Thus the first method of expanding a topic—by partition—is given a brief sentence or two of explanation and six different illustrations. Here Erasmus is at his favorite task of making available to readers of his day selected passages of classical literature.

The problem of organizing his subject for the convenience of the student is less to his liking. The numbered chapters of Book I have given way to a series of numbered methods of varying or expanding a theme. But this breaks down in the course of the eleventh method—

the accumulation of proofs. By an easy transition from commonplaces Erasmus arrives at the exemplum and to this favorite device of the medieval preacher he devotes more than half of Book II. Among numerous subdivisions of this section appears one explaining how a student should collect and classify in his notebook exempla from his reading of classical authors for use in his own writing. For good measure Erasmus illustrates his directions with a discourse on the death of Socrates, another on sailing, and a third, several pages in length, on the theme of inconstancy. Perhaps reminded by this theme of what he is supposed to be doing, he remarks that he will now continue with the methods of enlarging upon a topic. But the plan with which he had begun Book II having long since gone by the boards, he presents but one more method—multiplication of the parts of an oration. He then brings his work to a close with some suggestions on what a student of copia should avoid. It is to be presumed that the engaging style of Book II of the *De copia* served to compensate for its at times unsystematic approach.

Much of the illustrative material, which constitutes by far the largest part of Book II, is not original with Erasmus. He does not always quote directly from the works of the author from whom he is borrowing, nor does he habitually give an indication of the source of his quotation. At times he quotes page after page from a series of authors, often without any hint that the material is not his own. A list of the writers most often quoted in the two books of the *De copia* includes: Apuleius, Aristophanes, Aulus Gellius, Cicero, Euripides, Homer, Horace, Livy, Lucian, Macrobius, Martial, Ovid, Persius, Plautus, Quintilian, Sallust, St. Jerome, Seneca, Terence, Varro and Vergil. Of these names the most important are Quintilian, from whose work come about seventy of a total of more than one hundred and fifty citations, and Cicero, whose writings supply (either directly or through quotation from Quintilian's quotations of his work) a greater number of illustrations for the *De copia* than do those of any other single author.

IV.   The Importance of the *De copia*

In his lengthy study of the school curriculum in Shakespeare's age, T. W. Baldwin[7] discusses at great length the important place of the *De copia* in the educational pattern of the time. The schoolmasters' editions and commentaries that began to appear even in Erasmus' lifetime provide further evidence of Erasmus' impact on Renaissance education. In 1526, a schoolmaster, Georg Major (1502-1574) reduced

---

[7] T. W. Baldwin, *Wm. Shakespeare's Small Latine and Lesse Greeke*, (Urbana, Illinois: University of Illinois Press, 1944).

chapters 11 to 32 of Book I and all of Book II to a set of tables that could be printed in twelve or fifteen octavo pages. This summary of the *De copia* was first printed as part of a text which included the same author's summary of a rhetoric by Melanchthon and a digest of the tropes and schemes prepared by Petrus Mosellanus. This little textbook proved popular for the next half century. In 1527 there appeared another treatment of the methods of varying. This time an anonymous author expanded chapters 11 to 32 of Book I into something more than three times their original length, while calling his book an epitome of the copia of words. The epitome was frequently published as an appendage to the *De copia*.

Still another schoolmaster, M. Veltkirchius, prepared an even more ambitious work on the *De copia*. After each of the first thirty-two chapters of Book I and all of the sections of Book II he added a brief summary of the text and explained the rhetorical terms and classical allusions. This commentary of Veltkirchius when published separately made a book more than half as long as the *De copia* itself; usually, however, it was integrated with the text of Erasmus. It first appeared in 1534 from a press in Hagenau, the manuscript having been delivered to the printer by Melanchthon after the death of Veltkirchius who had been his friend.

In addition to its influence in the schools of the sixteenth century, the *De copia* has another importance. In his study of Renaissance humanism, R. R. Bolgar[8] says:

> The *De copia* has not been accorded the importance it deserves. It provides us in a sense with a clue to the whole of Humanism. Specifying the techniques on which imitation depended, it makes clear what men were attempting not only in Latin, but also in the vernaculars. . . .
> If we want to trace how the Humanist practice of imitation affected creative writing, if we want to go behind the scenes and cast on eye on the mechanism of the process . . . our best guide is Erasmus. . . . The *De copia* . . . outlines his method. The *Adages* presents us with the fruits of that method. . . . And finally the *Colloquies* and the *Praise of Folly* show us the finished product.

It is to be hoped that the present translation will make more widely available the contents of this book so fundamental to an understanding of both the literature and the educational methods of the Renaissance.

This volume includes a translation of the first thirty-three chapters of Book I and all of Book II. A number of illustrative phrases or formulae have been omitted from Book I, particularly those which have

[8] R. R. Bolgar, *The Classical Heritage and its Beneficiaries*, (Cambridge: Cambridge University Press, 1954), pp. 273-75.

[7]

significance only in their original Latin. Also omitted are the two hundred variations on the second of the two sentences at the end of Chapter 33 mentioned above. In Book II a relatively small number of illustrative examples have not been translated, but only in cases where it was felt that enough examples of the point in question have been given for twentieth century readers.

We should like to acknowledge our indebtedness to Miss Katherine Stokes, formerly of the Pennsylvania State University Library and now at Western Michigan College, for her patient help in solving many of the library problems connected with this work. We would like also to thank the Pennsylvania State University Council on Research for a grant of money to help carry out this project. Finally, special thanks are due to Louise King, who typed and retyped the manuscript.

In the preparation of this book the first of the two men whose names appear below was chiefly responsible for the translation, the second for the bibliographical work and the collation of the text.

DONALD B. KING
H. DAVID RIX

Note to the Reader

The technical vocabulary of the sixteenth century in matters rhetorical far surpassed that of the twentieth century in the number and
subtlety of its distinctions. In particular, the vast array of special names
assigned to the various figures of speech can be very confusing to the
modern reader, even the scholar. Some of these names have no exact
counterpart in modern English. In this translation, the names of the
figures have been translated when there is a modern equivalent in ordinary usage; in other cases the Latin name has been retained. The
"Index of Figures" at the back of the translation shows the page on
which the reader will find Erasmus' own definition of each figure.

The word copia presents a special problem. Weltkirch, a sixteenth
century Erasmian commentator, defined copia as the "faculty of varying the same expression or thought in many ways by means of different
forms of speech and a variety of figures and arguments. Copia of words
has its origins in grammar; copia of thought, in dialectic." However,
the word is used by Erasmus to denote not only the faculty of varying,
but also varying itself. Indeed, as used by Erasmus, copia encompasses
within its meaning the meaning of four English words: *variation*,
abundance or richness, *eloquence*, and the *ability* to vary or enrich
language and thought. In view of the impossibility of finding a suitable
English word to translate it, the word copia has been used as an English
word throughout the text of the translation.

In physical matters, the translation reflects insofar as possible the
order and arrangement of the original. The paragraphing, presentation
of examples, and the punctuation, where possible without confusion,
are as Erasmus had them.

D.B.K.

Desiderius Erasmus of Rotterdam
ON COPIA OF WORDS

BOOK I

CHAPTER I

That the Aspiration to Copia Is Dangerous

Just as there is nothing more admirable or more splendid than a speech with a rich copia of thoughts and words overflowing in a golden stream, so it is, assuredly, such a thing as may be striven for at no slight risk, because, according to the proverb,

Not every man has the luck to go to Corinth.[1]

Whence we see it befalls not a few mortals that they strive for this divine excellence diligently, indeed, but unsuccessfully, and fall into a kind of futile and amorphous loquacity, as with a multitude of inane thoughts and words thrown together without discrimination, they alike obscure the subject and burden the ears of their wretched hearers. To such a degree is this true that a number of writers, having gone so far as to deliver precepts concerning this very thing, if it please the gods, seem to have accomplished nothing else than, having professed copia (abundance) to have betrayed their poverty. And in truth this thing has so disturbed us, that partly selecting those from among the precepts of the art of Rhetoric suitable to this purpose, and partly adapting those which we have learned by a now long-continued experience in speaking and writing and have observed in our varied reading of a great many authors, we here set forth concerning each kind of copia, a number of principles, examples, and rules. We have not, to be sure, attempted to cover everything fully in a book, but have been content, in the publication of what one might call a brief treatise, to have opened the way to the learned and studious, and as it were to have furnished certain raw materials for other workers in the field. We have thus limited our efforts partly because we were moved to undertake this labor solely by the desire to be of service and do not begrudge all the glory going to another if only we have produced something useful to youth eager for knowledge, and partly because we

Many passages from the writings of ancient authors which Erasmus quoted as illustrations or examples, he repeated from the works of Quintilian or another, instead of directly from the works of the original author. In these notes, ref-erences to such secondary sources are enclosed in parentheses immediately following references to the primary sources.

[1] Horace *Epistles* i. 17, 36. Cf. Aulus Gellius *Attic Nights* i. 8, 4.

have been devoted to more serious studies to an extent that there is lacking very much leisure to spend on these lesser ones, most useful to be sure to the former kind, indeed of the greatest use, but nevertheless minute in themselves.

CHAPTER II

By Whom Copia Was Developed and by Whom Practiced

Further, lest anyone think this a modern device and to be disdained as lately born at our home, let him know that this method of diversifying speech is touched on lightly in a number of places by a very learned and likewise very diligent man, Quintilian,[2] and that many noted Sophists showed the way to the advantages of condensing speech. And they would not by any means have been able to do this without pointing out also a method of amplification; and if their books were extant, or if, as Quintilian suggests,[3] they had been willing to expound their doctrines fully, there would have been no need at all for these modest precepts of mine. It is a further recommendation of this thing that eminent men in every branch of learning have eagerly and diligently practiced this one. Thus there still survive several admirable efforts of Vergil about a mirror, about a stream frozen by the cold, about Iris, about the rising of the sun, about the four seasons of the year, about the heavenly constellations. That Aesopic fable about the fox and the crow which Apuleius narrates briefly with a wonderful economy of words, and also amplifies as fully as possible with a great many words, doubtless to exercise and display his genius, shows the same thing fully.[4] But come, who could find fault with this study when he sees that Cicero, that father of all eloquence, was so given to this exercise that he used to compete with his friend, the mimic actor, Roscius, to see whether the latter might express the same idea more times by means of various gestures, or he himself render it more often in speech varied through copia of eloquence.

[2] See Quintilian *Education of an Orator* (hereinafter referred to as Quintilian) viii. 2; xii. 1; and in general, Books viii, ix and x.

[3] Quintilian iii. 1, 21.

[4] Apuleius *Prologue* to *On the God of Socrates* 4.

Chapter III

How Authors Have Indulged in a Display of Copia

Moreover, the same authors, not only in school, but also in their serious work, sometimes indulged in a display of copia; while they at one time so compress a subject that you can take nothing away, at another, they so enrich and expand the same subject that you can add nothing to it. Homer, according to Quintilian,[5] is equally admirable at both—now copia, now brevity. Although it is not our intention here to cite examples, yet we will cite one of each from the peerless Vergil. What can have been said by anyone more concisely than this: "And the fields, where Troy was"?[6] With the fewest words, as Macrobius says, he consumed the state and engulfed it; not even a ruin was left.[7] On the other hand, listen to how fully he has treated the same topic:

> The final day has come and the inescapable doom
> Of Troy; we were Trojans, there was Ilium and a great
> Glory of the Trojans, cruel Jupiter Argos, all has
> Taken away: the Greeks are supreme in a burning city.
> O fatherland, O home of the gods, Ilium, and Trojans'
> Walls, famed in war. . . .
> Who the disaster of that night, who the sorrows in words
> Could express? or who could make its tears equal to
> its sufferings?[8]

What fountain, what torrent, what sea has overflowed with as many waves as he has with words? But it might appear that this example should rather be referred to copia of thought. He indulged in profusion of words also when he said:

> . . . . Does he survive and breathe the upper air,
> Nor yet lie dead in the cruel shadows?[9]

But this thing is more common in Ovid, to such a degree that he is criticized on the score that he does not preserve due moderation in copia. However, he is criticized by Seneca, whose whole style Quintilian, Suetonius and Aulus Gellius condemn.[10]

---

[5] Quintilian x. 1, 46.
[6] Vergil *Aeneid* iii. 11.
[7] Macrobius *Saturnalia* v. 1.
[8] Vergil *Aeneid* ii. 324-27; 241-42; 361- 62.
[9] Vergil *Aeneid* i, 546-47.
[10] Quintilian x. 1, 125. Aulus Gellius *Attic Nights* xiii 2. 2.

CHAPTER IV

To Whom Unrestrained Copia Has Been
Attributed As a Fault

Nor does it matter to me that some writers have been criticized for unduly and mistakenly striving for copia. For Quintilian notes too effusive and redundant copia in Stesichorus; but he mentions it in such a way as to confess that the fault should not be entirely avoided.[11] In Old Comedy Aeschylus is reproached because he said the same thing twice. "ἥκω καὶ κατέρχομαι," that is, I am come back and I am returned.[12] Seneca scarcely tolerates Vergil's repeating the same idea two or three times.[13] And, not to needlessly recount a long list, there have not been lacking those who condemned even Cicero as Asian and redundant and too extravagant in copia.[14] But these things, as I said, don't at all concern me, who indeed am not prescribing how one should write and speak, but am pointing out what to do for training, where, as everyone knows, all things ought to be exaggerated. Then I am instructing youth, in whom extravagance of speech does not seem wrong to Quintilian, because with judgment, superfluities are easily restrained, certain of them even, age itself wears away, while on the other hand, you cannot by any method cure meagerness and poverty.[15]

CHAPTER V

That It Is Characteristic of the Same Artist to
Speak Both Concisely and Copiously

Now if there are any who fully approve the Homeric Menelaus, a man of few words, and who, on the other hand, disapprove of Ulysses, rushing on like a river swollen by the winter snows, that is, those whom laconism and conciseness greatly delight, not even they ought to object to our work, for in fact they themselves would find it not unprofitable, because it seems best to proceed by the same principle either to speak most concisely or most fully. If indeed it is true, as in Plato, Socrates acutely reasons, that the ability to lie and to tell the truth cleverly are talents of the same man, no artist will better compress speech to conciseness than he who has skill to enrich the same with as varied an ornamentation as possible. For as far as conciseness of

---

[11] Quintilian x. 1, 62.
[12] Aristophanes *Frogs* 1154 *seq.*
[13] Aulus Gellius *Attic Nights* xii. 2, 2.

[14] Quintilian xii. 10, 12 *ad fin.*
[15] Quintilian ii. 4. 5 *seq.*

speech is concerned, who could speak more tersely than he who has ready at hand an extensive array of words and figures from which he can immediately select what is most suitable for conciseness? Or as far as concerns conciseness of thought, who would be more able at expressing any subject in the fewest possible words than one who has learned and studied what the matters of special importance in a case are, the supporting pillars, as it were, what are most closely related, what are appropriate for purposes of ornament. No one certainly will see more quickly and more surely what can be suitably omitted than he who has seen what can be added and in what ways.

CHAPTER VI

Concerning Those Who Strive for Either Conciseness or Copia Foolishly

But if we use either brevity or copia without method, there is the danger that there may befall us what we see happen to certain perverse affectors of laconism, although they speak but few words, yet even in those few, many, not to say all, are superfluous.[16] Just as in a different way it may happen to those who unskillfully strive for copia that although they are excessively loquacious, yet they say too little, leaving out many things that certainly need to be said.

Accordingly, our precepts will be directed to this, that you may be able in the fewest possible words so to comprehend the essence of a matter that nothing is lacking; that you may be able to amplify by copia in such a way that there is nonetheless no redundancy; and, the principle learned, that you may be free either to emulate laconism, if you wish, or to copy Asian exuberance, or to exhibit Rhodian moderation.

CHAPTER VII

That Copia Is Twofold

Furthermore, I think it is clear that copia is twofold, as Quintilian himself declares, especially admiring among the other excellences of Pindar that most happy copia of thought and words.[17] And of these one consists in *Synonymia*, in *Heterosis* or *Enallage* of words, in metaphor, in change of word form, in *Isodynamia* and the remaining ways

[16] See Quintilian viii. 3, 56, on κακοζήλια, excellence carried to ex- cess. [17] Quintilian x. 1. 61.

of this sort for gaining variety; the other depends upon the piling up, expanding and amplifying of arguments, *exempla, collationes,* similes, *dissimilia, contraria,* and other methods of this sort, which we will discuss in more detail in their proper place. Although these can be observed anywhere, so closely combined that you cannot tell them apart at all easily, so much does one serve the other, so that they might seem to be distinct only in theory, rather than in fact and in use, nevertheless, for the purpose of teaching, we shall make the distinction in such a way that we cannot deservedly be condemned for hair splitting in distinguishing, nor, on the other hand, for negligence.

Chapter VIII

For What Things This Training Is Useful

Now in order that studious youth may apply itself to this study with an eager disposition we shall make clear in a few words for what things it is of use. First of all then, this training in varying speech will be useful in every way for attaining good style, which is a matter of no little moment. In particular, however, it will be useful in avoiding tautology, that is, repetition of the same word or expression, a vice not only unseemly but also offensive. It not infrequently happens that we have to say the same thing several times, in which case, if destitute of copia we will either be at a loss, or, like the cuckoo, croak out the same words repeatedly, and be unable to give different shape or form to the thought. And thus betraying our want of eloquence we will appear ridiculous ourselves and utterly exhaust our wretched audience with weariness. Worse than tautology is *homologia,* as Quintilian says,[18] which does not lighten tedium with any charm of variety, and is wholly monotonous. Moreover, who is so patient a listener that he would even for a short time put up with a speech unvarying throughout? Variety everywhere has such force that nothing at all is so polished as not to seem rough when lacking its excellence. Nature herself especially rejoices in variety; in such a great throng of things she has left nothing anywhere not painted with some wonderful artifice of variety. And just as the eye is held more by a varying scene, in the same way the mind always eagerly examines whatever it sees as new. And if all things continually present themselves to the mind without variation, it will at once turn away in disgust. Thus the whole profit of a speech is lost. This great fault he will shun easily who is prepared to turn the same thought into many forms, as the famous Proteus is said to have

18 Quintilian viii. 3. 52.

changed his form. And in truth this training will contribute greatly to skill in extemporaneous speaking or writing; it will assure that we will not frequently hesitate in bewilderment or keep shamefully silent. Nor will it be difficult, with so many formulas prepared in readiness for action, to aptly divert even a rashly begun speech in any desired direction. Besides, in interpreting authors, in translating books from a foreign language, in writing verse, it will give us no little help, since in such matters, unless we are trained in the principles of copia, we shall often find ourselves either confused, or crude, or even silent.

CHAPTER IX

By What Methods of Training This Faculty May Be Developed

Next it remains to mention briefly by what methods of training this faculty may be developed. Having diligently committed the precepts to memory, we should often of set purpose select certain expressions and make as many variations of them as possible in the way Quintilian advises, "just as several different figures are commonly formed from the same piece of wax."[19] This work, moreover, will bear richer fruit, if several students compete with one another either orally or in writing, on a subject set for them. For then each individual will be aided by their common discoveries, and, the opportunity having been furnished, each one will discover many things. Again, we may treat some theme as a whole in many ways. And in this matter it will be well to emulate the ingenuity of Milo of Croton, so that making at first two variations, then three, then more and more, we may attain to such ability that at length we can without difficulty make a hundred or two hundred variations. In addition we will greatly increase the copia of our speech by translation from Greek authors, because the Greek language is especially rich in both word and thought. Moreover, it will occasionally be very useful to emulate them by paraphrasing. It will be of especial help to rewrite the verses of poets in prose; and on the other hand, to bind prose in meter, and put the same theme into first one and then another type of verse. And it will be very helpful for us to emulate and attempt by our own efforts to equal or even to improve upon that passage in any author which appears unusually rich in copia. Moreover, it will be especially useful if we peruse good authors night and day, particularly those who have excelled in copia of speech, such as Cicero, Aulus Gellius, Apuleius; and with vigilant eyes we should note

[19] Quintilian x. 5. 9.

all figures in them, store up in our memory what we have noted, imitate what we have stored up, and by frequent use make it a habit to have them ready at hand.

CHAPTER X

First Precept Concerning Copia

Having said these things as a sort of preface, it remains to address ourselves to the propounding of precepts, although the things we have already said can be regarded as precepts. However, it does not seem that we will be acting illogically if we commence the precepts here by forewarning the student of copia that, above all, care must be taken that speech be appropriate, be Latin, be elegant, be correct; and that he should not consider anything to belong to copia that is not consistent with the purity of the Roman language.

Elegance consists partly in words used by suitable authors; partly in using the right word; and partly in using it in the right expression. What clothing is to our body, diction is to the expression of our thoughts. For just as the fine appearance and dignity of the body are either set off to advantage or disfigured by dress and habit, just so thought is by words. Accordingly, they err greatly who think that it matters nothing in what words something is expressed, provided only it is in some way understandable. And the reason for changing clothes and for varying speech is one and the same. Consequently, let this be the primary concern, that the clothes be not dirty, or ill fitting, or improperly arranged. For it would be a shame if a figure good in itself should be displeasing because degraded by dirty clothes. And it would be ridiculous for a man to appear in public in a woman's dress, and unseemly for anyone to be seen with his clothes turned backside to and inside out. Therefore, if anyone should wish to strive for copia before he has acquired competence in the Latin language, that one, in my opinion at least, would be acting no less ridiculously than a pauper who did not own a single garment that he could wear without great shame, and who, suddenly changing his clothes, should appear in the forum covered by assorted rags, ostentatiously exhibiting his poverty instead of his riches. And will he not appear more senseless the more often he does this? I think he will. And yet no less absurdly do some of those who strive for copia act, who, although they are not able to express their thoughts even in one way in elegant phrases, nevertheless, just as if they were ashamed to appear insufficiently stammering, variously rephrase their stuttering in such a way as to make it more stuttering; as if they have undertaken a contest with themselves to speak as barbarously as possible. I want the furnishings of a rich house to exhibit the greatest variety; but I want it to be altogether in good taste, not with every corner crammed with willow and fig and Samian ware. At a splendid banquet I want various kinds of food to be served, but who could endure anyone serving a hundred different dishes not one of which but would move to nausea? I have deliberately given this warning at length, because I know the rash presumption of very many people who prefer to omit the fundamentals and (as the saying goes) with dirty feet to hasten to the heights straightway. Nor do they sin much less seriously who, mixing the sordid with the elegant, disfigure the purple with rags, and intersperse glass among precious stones, and combine garlic with Attic sweetmeats. Now we shall set forth formulas for varying, those of course that pertain to copia of words.

CHAPTER XI

The First Method of Varying by *Synonymia*

The first, then, and simplest method of varying depends upon those words which, although they are different, express exactly the same thought, so that as far as the meaning goes it makes no difference whether you choose rather to use one or the other. And these, indeed, are called synonyms by the grammarians, the opposite of what are called homonyms. Some venture to call the former univocal; the latter, equivocal, although according to the logicians these terms correspond with the ideas themselves better than they do with the names. For we should correctly call different words meaning the same thing ἰσοδυναμοῦσαι and the opposite of these πολυσημοι. Of the first type are *ensis* (brand), *gladius* (sword); *domus* (house), *aedes* (building); *codex* (book), *liber* (book); *forma* (beauty), *decor* (comeliness), *pulchritudo* (loveliness). Accordingly, the greatest number of these must be drawn from good authors everywhere—a varied furniture, or (as Quintilian says) riches piled up, so that whenever it is desirable there may be available for us a supply of words.[20] Nor will it be sufficient to have prepared an abundant supply and rich store of such words unless you have them not only ready, but in sight, so that even without being sought they may come instantly to mind. Yet in this matter, we must be especially careful not to say (as some do) at just any point, whatever first comes to mind, indiscriminately, as if taking it from a heap. For in the first place, scarcely anywhere will you find two words so close in meaning that they do not differ in some respect.

[20] Quintilian x. 1. 5.

For what has so much the same meaning as *homines* (men) and *mortales* (mortals)? And yet that Greek proverb, *sweet oil on lentils,* applies to anyone who indiscriminately uses *omnes mortales* (all mortals) for *omnes homines* (all men). In some places *letter* and *epistle* have the same meaning; in other places, different meanings. Then, although we grant there to be no difference at all in meaning, yet some words are more becoming than others, more exalted, more polished, more humorous, more emphatic, more sonorous, more suited to composition. Accordingly, discrimination should be exercised by one who is going to speak, so that from all, he chooses the best words. In selecting, judgment is required; in storing away, diligence. A careful observance of the niceties and peculiarities of speech will assure that you have judgment; constant reading of authors of every kind will permit you to store up as many words as possible, since poets express things in certain words, and orators in others. And some words are peculiar to certain ages and times. In truth even the same authors often express the same thing in different ways. First, then, the best possible words must be selected from every type of writer. Next, whatever kind they are, they will be added to the collection, and no word is to be rejected provided only it be found in some writer not entirely bad. For there is no word that is not the best in some place. Consequently, however low it be, however unusual, poetic, archaic, new, obsolete, harsh, barbarous, and exotic, nevertheless, let it be placed in its own company, as it were, and nest, so that if ever a need for it arise, it may be summoned then. But if we are afraid that the novelty or archaism of a word may be offensive to listeners, it will be well to make use of Quintilian's advice that we remember to prepare them for it in advance.[21] That may be done commonly by phrases like these: Cato, the gormandizer of books, if yet it is right to use such a word for so elevated a matter; to speak in the manner of Plautus; for why should I not use words of Ennius?; for gladly we use a Horatian word, for thus those moderns speak; you recognize a word of the camp; as the poets say; as the ancients used to say; to speak like the ancients; if it is permitted to speak thus; if you permit me to speak in the popular manner; for I shall speak in Greek, that I may speak better. The same thing must be done with those words that are called risqué, i.e., which border on the obscene in meaning.

Low Words

Low words, then, are those that will appear meaner than befits the dignity of the subject, as if one should call a friend and familiar, a pal. Of this class for the most part are those taken from the meaner

21 Quintilian viii. 3. 37.

crafts and trades, such as the baths, the kitchens, the tanneries, the cookshops. And yet we use these of necessity when such subjects are to be discussed. For surgeons and doctors are compelled at times to use words fitting rather than fine, and Pliny jests in camp language. Moreover, some words are base in themselves, others in reference to a subject, or persons, or other circumstances; for instance, *stercus* (manure) and *stercorare* (to manure) are not base words if one should use them in talking about agriculture among farmers; but they are, if one is talking before a prince about the republic.

UNUSUAL WORDS

In former times the chief authority was with public usage, as Horace bears witness:

Many words will be born again that now are dead,
And many will die that now are honored—if usage wills.[22]

In these times, since the rules of speech are sought not from the multitude, but from the works of the learned, usage does not have the same authority. Nevertheless, unusual words can now and then be found in those authors that are very often read by the learned. And today we should be careful to avoid affected speech and to avoid the practice of those who think speaking unusually is speaking rightly, a trait Cicero notes in L. Lisenna,[23] a man competent in other respects, and of those who (as it is neatly put by Diomedes) only think themselves geniuses if there is need of a genius to understand them,[24] and finally of those who prefer to write what men wonder at rather than understand. Now this unusualness of speech can be achieved in more than one way as will be clear from what follows.

POETIC WORDS

There are in the poets, too, words that are to be used rather sparingly, especially in prose.

ARCHAIC WORDS

Archaic words add pleasure if they are interwoven moderately and suitably like ornaments.

OBSOLETE WORDS

Unusual words are those which are used only rarely; archaic words, those taken from writings abandoned by posterity on account of their age, as those from the XII Tables, from Ennius, Lucilius, Naevius, and Pacuvius. Obsolete words are those that have vanished completely into disuse and oblivion. Anyone who tried to speak in that way now would

[22] Horace *Art of Poetry* 70-71.   [24] Quintilian viii. Pr. 25.
[23] Cicero *On the Orator* i. 3. 12.

be ridiculous. I do not think there is any place for obsolete words, except in joking or irony. In this matter not only must the factor of age be considered, but also that of desire and inclination. For there can be seen after the age of Livius Andronicus an archaic style, now obsolete•and unused, which was gradually improved until the time of Cicero, when Roman eloquence became so polished that at last it could not become more so, but thence forward (as with all human affairs) degenerated from the peak of its brilliance. For later ages since they tried to speak differently, necessarily spoke worse. Nevertheless, Sallust, although he wrote in the same age as Cicero, is more like Cato the Censor than Cicero; and Maecenas, although he was nearly contemporaneous, yet was very far from the purity of his time. Likewise, Valerius Maximus, although he lived in the age of Tiberius Caesar when the brilliance of the time of Cicero had not yet been dimmed, nevertheless wrote in his own style rather than in that of his time. I will say nothing of Tacitus, Suetonius, Pliny, Aelius Lampridius, and other later men. But just as I approve the practice of those who are disposed to imitation of the former most fruitful age, so I do not approve some who shudder at what they find in these later writers as barbarous, especially since it is possible that what they flee here was in Cicero, in books that we do not have.

HARSH WORDS

Harsh words are those that are improperly used in a figurative sense. He has been censured who said that the republic was castrated by the death of Camillus, when he meant that the strength of the state failed with the death of that man.[25] And Horace rightly censures a certain Furius because he wrote: "Jupiter spit hoary snow all over the wintry Alps."[26] A similar example would be: he destroyed fields of peace; he stirred up mountains of war. It would have been less harsh had he taken a metaphor from the calm and the disturbed sea.

FOREIGN WORDS

Foreign words have their charm when used in the proper place.

OBSCENE WORDS

Obscene words ought to be far from all speech of Christians. No attention should be paid to the Cynics who do not think that it is shameful to say anything that it is not shameful to do; and that what is not shameful to do in private, it is not shameful to do in public, such as urinating or relieving the bowels. But, on the contrary, it is not always shameful to say what it is shameful to do. Parricide and

[25] Cicero *On the Orator* iii. 41. 164 (Quintilian viii. 6. 15).　　[26] Horace *Satires* ii. 5. 39-41 (Quintilian viii. 6. 17).

incest are mentioned without shame, although each is most shameful to commit. But, as there are certain parts of the body which, although not indecent of themselves, nevertheless are covered through a certain human modesty, so there are certain indifferent actions that are concealed out of modesty. But not always is it unseemly to designate by its name something it is indecorous to do publicly. To give birth is said with modesty, a thing, nevertheless, it would be disgraceful to do in public. It is modest to say stomach, but immodest to show it. Whence then is derived a rule of obscenity? From nowhere else but from the usage, not of anyone whatsoever, but of those whose speech is chaste. For the poets, especially the satirists, have permitted themselves too much in these matters. Sometimes a metaphor is more obscene than a simple word. Some words are twisted to an obscene meaning although they are decent in themselves. Accordingly, words that are manifestly obscene should be completely avoided. Those that are indifferent can be applied in a decent sense.

NEW WORDS

Three kinds of new words are acceptable: those that are new coinage, or those that are used in a new way, or those that are invented by compounding. And they have a charm if only they are interspersed in moderation and in the proper place. For as it has been neatly said by Quintilian: "Occasional sourness is pleasant in foods."[27] Furthermore, Greek words suitably intermingled with Latin add no slight charm. It is proper to use them either when the Greek word is more expressive, or more concise, or more emphatic, or more charming, or when we are making fun of a passage or a saying of some author. Finally, when we do not wish what we say to be understood by everyone and, not to pursue details, whenever some advantage ensues, we may interweave Greek words among the Latin, especially when we write for the learned. Otherwise, when no advantage does arise, one may excuse in schoolboys the practice of composing half in Latin and half in Greek in the traditional manner to develop their facility in both languages; but in men, in my opinion, this sort of display would be unseemly, and as lacking in dignity as if someone should alternately mix prose and meter in a book, although we know this has been done by certain learned men, for instance, by Petronius Arbiter, not however, without the appearance of madness; by Seneca, in a ludicrous encomium of Claudius; and, a work which is to be more admired, by Boethius, in serious argument.[28] And yet the latter was so unlike himself in his verses that scholars can scarcely believe that they were

[27] Quintilian vi. 3. 19.
[28] Petronius *Satyricon;* Seneca *Apocolo-* *cyntosis of Claudius;* Boethius *Consolation of Philosophy.*

written by his own unaided efforts. John Gerson, a writer not to be scorned if he had lived in this age, imitated Boethius.[29] It may be also that occasionally we will be forced to express what we think by a long circumlocution or borrowing from the Greeks. Then there are not a few words of the Greeks that long use has made Latin. To use these as if Latin will be permissible, for example: *rhetor, orator*, etc. Some of these are so customary that the Latin word is lacking, as: *philosophus, theologus, grammatica*, etc. Even in these there will be some variety if they are inflected sometimes in the Greek and sometimes in the Latin form.

Chapter XII
The Words Peculiar to Different Ages

And also it will be useful to observe how a particular age has achieved variety in the use of words. Cicero first dared to say *beatudinem* (blessedness) and *beatitatem* (blessedness); *aedituus* for *aeditimus* (temple keeper) was new in the age of Varro.[30] A collection of effective words of this type, what the Greeks call συναθροισμός, will be profitable not only in avoiding ὁμοιολογία, that is, the same style of speech everywhere, if it is ever necessary to repeat the same thing several times, but also in producing the vehemence necessary for δείνωσις, i.e., indignant emphasis: He went away, he broke out, he departed, he escaped;[31] you have slain your parent, you have killed your father, you have murdered your progenitor. And rhetors place this type among the ornaments of speech and call it *interpretatio*. I think it should be used as an exercise rather than in a speech. For it is a most difficult type of varying, the nature of the speech remaining the same, to habitually express the same meaning repeatedly, now in some words, now in others just as effective; for example, to risk danger, to undergo risk, to incur peril, to assume risk; he builds a house, he erects a dwelling; he bought a book, he purchased a manuscript; he sent away the boy, he dismissed the servant; you are held in such honor by him, you are so esteemed by him; I gained this prize, I won these rewards; he condoned the error, he forgave the offence, he pardoned the fault; as often as I recollect this day, as often as I recall, as often as I remember. Nothing is more distasteful to human ears, and Horace rightly enjoins:

> Let the thought move quickly
> Lest it encumber weary ears with onerous words.[32]

[29] Gerson *On the Consolation of Theology*.

[30] Cicero *On the Nature of the Gods* i. 34. 95. Varro *On Agriculture* i. 2.

[31] Cicero *Against Catiline* 2. 1. 1 (Quintilian ix. 3. 46).

[32] Horace *Satires* i. 10. 9.

It is otherwise when *iteratio* serves to convey an appeal to the emotions and some variety lightens the tedium of repetition. An example is this passage of Vergil's:

> ... Does he survive and breath the upper air,
> Nor yet lie dead in the cruel shadows?[33]

Similar to this is that copia of Cicero in defense of Quintus Ligarius: "O wonderful clemency, worthy of being honored by every praise and commendation, by literary works and monuments, etc."[34] He said similar things, not identical ones. Another passage in the same oration is praised, and deservedly, because it emphasizes the same thought in different words: "For when that sword of yours, Tubero, was unsheathed on the field of Pharsalus, what, etc."[35] I put forward this warning the more earnestly because I have observed that otherwise distinguished orators, especially among the Italians, cultivate this as if admirable, so that they waste time with synonyms of this sort; for example, if someone expounding this verse of the Psalmist, *Make a clean heart in me, God*, should speak thus: "Make in me a clean heart, a fine heart, a shining heart, an immaculate heart, a heart free from uncleanness, a heart defiled by no vice, a heart cleansed, a heart washed, a heart snow-white," and also might express the same thing in other words; this copia is not far from babbling.

CHAPTER XIII

Method of Varying by *Enallage or* Ἑτέρωσις

The next method of varying is when something of variety is gained by a small change in the same word, as: voracious, I devour; drinker, drunkard; fond of drink, I drink; talkative, talker; jest, I jest; babbler, I babble; fallacious, false; pleasurable, pleasant. Changing a noun substantive to an adjective or *vice versa* are in this category; for example, according to the expression of Homer, according to the Homeric expression; a man unusually eloquent, a man of unusual eloquence; extraordinarily impudent, of extraordinary impudence. Changing an active verb to a passive or *vice versa*: I am most grateful, the deepest gratitude toward you is felt by me; a great admiration possesses me, I am possessed by great admiration; not thus does a mother love her son, not thus is a son loved by his mother. And, to summarily state a thing infinitely various, this changing consists in two methods chiefly, either in changing the part of speech itself, or in keeping the same

[33] Vergil *Aeneid* i. 546-47.
[34] Cicero *For Ligarius* 2. *ad. fin.*
[35] Cicero *For Ligarius* 3. 9 (Quintilian viii. 4. 27).

[25]

part of speech and changing its form. And there are as many possible ways of changing as there are grammatical forms of a word. An example of the first method: I doubt not but that he is able. I have no doubt that he possesses ability. An infinitive in place of a noun: Virtue is to flee from vice, that is, virtue is flight from vice. In this expression a verb is interchanged with a noun: Love your lover; love him who loves you. Likewise, a verb is interchanged with a participle, a verb is substituted for a supine or participle, a gerundive is changed to a gerund, an infinitive replaces a participle, a noun is used for a gerund, a supine for a verb, an adverb is exchanged for a noun. But perhaps we shall speak more fully of these things on a more opportune occasion. Now, for the purposes of teaching let us write briefly about variation of form, pointing out clearly the exact sources.

NUMBER
Singular and plural are interchanged: the Roman victor in the battle, instead of Roman victors in the battles. In general, change of number is more frequent and less harsh in nouns which the grammarians call collective, such as: crowd, people, herd, series; or in those that indicate not some one individual, but a genus or species. For it does not matter whether you say: An elephant gives birth finally in the tenth year; or elephants give birth in the tenth year.

PERSON
Person is varied in many ways; the writer can select whichever one he wishes: what should you do? as man is, so you should act. To this class belongs the figure called apostrophe, when we address an oration to some person or to some thing as though to a person, as: He assassinates Polydore and seizes his gold by force. Cursed thirst of gold, to what do you not force the hearts of men?[36]

VOICE
There is some variety in change of voice: he laments, he is lamented.

CASE
Likewise case can be changed.

SPECIES
Species is varied when we use derivatives for the original form as: prevented by great affairs, prevented by the greatness of affairs; or when we use diminutives instead of the simple form, or frequentatives for primitive verbs, or a substantive for an adjective, or a patrony-

[36] Vergil *Aeneid* iii. 57 *seq.* (Quintilian
ix. 2. 10; ix. 3. 25).

[26]

mic for the root form. Although this would be permitted in poetry perhaps, in prose none would tolerate it.

FORM

Change of form aids copia whenever we use simple speech for compound or *vice versa;* and this may be done either with or without trope.

Tense, mood, declension and conjugation can also be varied.

CHAPTER XIV

Method of Varying by *Antonomasia*

The next method of varying speech is *antonomasia,* i.e., change of name, as: if one should say Aeacides or Pelides for Achilles; Romulides for Romans; Priamides or Dardanides for Trojans. Sometimes one may substitute an epithet for the name itself: Which the Impious left hanging in the chamber.[37] He used the Impious for Aeneas; Livy used Carthaginian for Hannibal. It is an example of the same type when one says the Poet, meaning Homer; the Philosopher meaning Aristotle; and in the same way the Greeks call the King of Persia the King. It is also of this type when one says Verres for a thief; Sardanapalus for an effeminate person; Croesus for a rich man, Phalerides for a cruel one; which things we shall discuss in their own place.

CHAPTER XV

Method of Varying by *Periphrasis*

If the *antonomasia* includes very many words it will be *periphrasis,* which some call *circuitio,* for example, if someone should say destroyer of Carthage and Numantia for Scipio;[38] or as Horace said, author of the *Trojan Wars* for Homer. Moreover, this method includes several types, *etymologia, notatio, finitio.*

Etymologia

It is *etymologia* when we indicate the origin of a name, as, if one should call a legacy hunter, he who strives for and obtains the inheritances of others; or for parasite should say a man devoted to food and his belly.

[37] Vergil *Aeneid iv.* 495-96 (Quintilian viii. 6).   [38] Quintilian viii. 6. 30.

Notatio

It is *notatio* when we describe any thing by certain of its distinctive features, as if someone feeling anger should speak of a boiling over of his spirit or bile which induced pallor in his countenance, fire in his eyes, trembling in his limbs. And it is of the same type when someone traces with his finger a head by which effeminate and unmanly men are indicated. Or if you should say, he blows his nose with his elbow, meaning he is a fish dealer.

Finitio

It is *finitio* when anyone calls rhetoric the art of speaking well; a peculator, a man who had plundered the state treasury; a tyrant, a man who had oppressed by force the laws and liberty of the citizens.

CHAPTER XVI

Method of Varying by Metaphor

Another method of varying comes from metaphor, which is called *translatio* (transference) in Latin because it transfers a word from its real and proper meaning to one not its own. This is done in many ways.

Deflexio

First by *deflexio*, as often as a word is transferred from a related thing to one very close, as, I see, for I understand. Nothing is more used than such a type of metaphor.

FROM THE IRRATIONAL TO THE RATIONAL

The next type is the transfer from the unreasoning animal to a being endowed with reason or vice versa. As if one should say that a man of odious and fatuous loquacity brayed, or bleated, or grunted, or barked.

FROM THE ANIMATE TO THE INANIMATE OR *Vice Versa*

The metaphor will be more difficult to find if it is a transference from the animate to the inanimate or *vice versa*: And now every field, every tree is in labor.[39]

FROM THE ANIMATE TO THE ANIMATE

As if someone should speak of pasturing bees.

FROM THE INANIMATE TO THE INANIMATE

This metaphor is used when one speaks of a forest welling up, which is an expression used of fountains.

[39] Vergil *Eclogues* 3. 56.

CHAPTER XVII

Reciprocal Metaphors

Certain metaphors are reciprocal or common. The Greeks call them ἀκόλουθα. For as you might say charioteer for pilot; so you might rightly say pilot for charioteer. Certain ones can be applied in only one way, the Greeks call them ἀνακόλουθα, i.e., not reciprocal. Since indeed as you rightly transfer crown (*vertex*) from man to mountain, so you would not properly refer summit (*cacumen*) to man. However, as Quintilian says, metaphor contributes not only to copia of speech by assuring that nothing will appear to be lacking a name, but also to ornamentation, dignity, vivid presentation, sublimity, humor.[40] And sometimes it is necessary, as the farmers speak of a gem on vines, of vines gemming, of fields thirsting, of fruit being afflicted, of crops being luxuriant, and we speak of a hard man, a rough one, for we have no other word.[41] But it is not within our present plan to pursue in more detail the number of ways metaphor may be used and to what degree it may differ from very closely related tropes. It will serve to suggest that whoever wishes to be more fluent in speech should observe and collect from the best authors a great number of striking metaphors and for the same purpose add many *similitudines*. The best are in Cicero; there are a great many in Quintilian. But in these matters hardly any other is more productive than Plutarch. From the *Adagia* likewise not a few can be collected because many contain an allegory or some sort of metaphor. In collecting these we labored, I know not how successfully, but certainly with great vigilance. Nothing indeed keeps us from forming metaphors ourselves by reading and by observing the nature of all things, provided only that the metaphor be not harsh, or low, or more exaggerated than is proper, or mixed, or too frequent, especially in the same class. It will likewise not be out of place to point out that a metaphor is sometimes found in a single noun, as if one should call a man devoted to his belly an animal; sometimes in an epithet, as when we speak of a man of stone, or an iron writer, or glassy waves, or a flowering age; sometimes in a single verb, as, a lifetime flies away, the years glide by; sometimes something is added to explain the metaphor, he inflamed the man with a passion for glory, he fired him with wrath.

[40] Quintilian viii. 6. 4.   [41] Quintilian viii. 6. 6.

[29]

CHAPTER XVIII

Method of Varying by Allegory

Allegory has the same force as metaphor. For allegory is nothing but a continuous metaphor, as: he would scuttle the ship in which he himself sails, i.e., he would overthrow the state, in the fall of which he himself must also perish. Use of this is more common in proverbial *sententiae* and in proverbs, as: flame is near smoke, which means that peril ought to be avoided in good time; saleable wine has no need of ivy trimmings, by which we mean, a thing praiseworthy in itself has no need of other recommendation. In proverbs of this sort, allegory sometimes results in enigma. Nor is that bad, if you are talking to the learned, or writing; indeed, in the latter case, not even if for the general reader. For things should not be written in such a way that everyone understands everything, but so that they are forced to investigate certain things, and learn.

CHAPTER XIX

Methods of Varying by *Catachresis*

Catachresis has the same force as the Latin term *abusio,* and is distinguished from metaphor by this characteristic, that it is *abusio* when we use a word to express a meaning related to its own for which no proper word already exists, but metaphor when such a word does exist. Just as when we call one who has killed his brother a parricide, because fratricide is not used; and there are no fish in the fish pond in which we bathe;[42] man's strength is brief; far reaching plan;[43] petty spirit, instead of small. Quintilian especially approves that type of speech in which the three-fold charm of *similitudo,* allegory and metaphor is mingled, as in Cicero: "What strait, what Euripus, do you think has so many movements, so great and so variable disturbances and changes of current as the disturbances and eddying currents in the affairs of the assemblies? Let a day elapse, or a night intervene and often everything is thrown into disorder, and a slight breath of rumor will sometimes change every opinion."[44]

The *similitudo* is developed and the metaphor adapted to what Cicero calls *collatio.* He burned all over with wrath, is a metaphor. Just as iron glows fiery with flame, so his whole countenance was in-

---

[42] The Latin word for a bathing pool is *piscina,* literally, a "fish pond."
[43] *Rhetoric for Herennius* iv. 33. 45.

[44] Cicero *For Murena* 17. 35 (Quintilian viii. 6. 49.

flamed with wrath, is *collatio*. And so, in that Cicero compares the waves of Euripus to the instability of the assemblies, it is *similitudo;* in that he says that it has waves, it is allegory; "a breath of rumor" is metaphor. However, these tropes pertain likewise to copia of thought, which we will discuss in the second book.

CHAPTER XX

Variation by Onomatopoeia

Some variety comes also from onomatopoeia, which can be called the coining of a name. Of this type are taratantara for the song of a bugle, hissing, murmur, rumbling. *Paragoge,* i.e., the development and derivation of new words by analogy, belongs in the same class. Why we should avoid this I do not see, if ever the thought demands it; and just as we say *cacaturire* (to desire to go to stool), *esurire* (to desire to eat), what is to prevent our saying by analogy *dormiturire* (to desire to sleep), *scripturire* (to desire to write). And just as we say Graecize, why should we not also say youthize, poetize, rhetoricize, philosophize, theologize? And the Greeks, indeed, are far more productive of these coinages than the Latins. So I think we ought to dare some, especially in verse and in translating Greek authors. Certainly those that are found in suitable authors should be confidently put to use. For we ought not to consider any word which may be found in an approved author harsh or obsolete. In this matter, indeed, I disagree completely with those who shudder at every word as barbaric that they have not read in Cicero. But in fact this observation should also be made, that sometimes there is a manifold *paragoge* of the same expression: *homunculus, homulus, homuncio* (mannikin). Observation of all these things will contribute not a little to copia of speech, because in these coined terms lies a great part of the wealth of the Latin language.

CHAPTER XXI

Method of Varying by *Metalepsis*

Similar to *abusio* is *metalepsis,* which is called *transumptio* by the Latins. This is when we proceed by steps to that which we wish to express, as: he hid in dark caves. For the connotation is of black caves, from black, obscure, and from this finally, extreme depth. Thus the Greeks call sharp what they wish to be thought swift. But a use for

[31]

this figure occurs more often in verse than in prose, and it can be considered a type of synecdoche just as those which follow.

CHAPTER XXII

Method of Varying by Metonymy

To no small degree does that trope which is called metonymy, i.e., the change of a name, make for copia of speech; and this is effected in many ways. Either when we use the originator for the thing in question, as in Vergil's "Ceres spoiled by the waters";[45] in Terence, "Venus is cold without Ceres and Bacchus";[46] in Horace: "Neptune received on land."[47] Here the originator or the protector is used for the thing in question; but if you should reverse this, it would be too harsh, as: let us pray to the vine. For here the god is present, here wine is used for Bacchus. Or when that which contains is employed for that which is contained, as: drained jugs; season most pleasing to heaven, i.e., to the heavenly ones; prosperous age. Or *vice versa,* which is more harsh and violent. Vergil: "Now, next to him Ucalegon burns."[48] He has used the man for his house. Terence: "let us go to us," i.e., to our homes.[49] And when we say of the man whose patrimony is used up, that he was consumed.[50] I pass on to you this one to be eaten up. Horace: "he tasted the old man," i.e., the money of the old man, where the master of the thing is used for the thing itself.[51] Or when we indicate the effect by the one effecting: he is faster than oars; for he means the speed which is gained by the oars. Or *vice versa,* as: sluggish cold, and, send gloomy fear, pale death,[52] bold youth. Or when we use the leader for those who are led, as when we speak of sixty thousand killed at Canna by Hannibal.[53] Or when we use the author for the work, as when we say, I have sold a Vergil; a Pliny always to be had in his hands.[54] It is similar to this when we speak of a sacrilege detected, not a sacrilegious man; and to have knowledge of arms, not of the science of arms.[55] To this class I think should be referred those terms that are used alike of persons and of things, as: eloquent man, eloquent speech; bold man, bold deed; you have confuted the man, you have confuted

[45] Vergil *Aeneid* i. 177 (Quintilian viii. 6. 23).
[46] Terence *Eunuch* iv. 5. 6.
[47] Horace *Art of Poetry* 63 (Quintilian viii. 6. 23).
[48] Vergil *Aeneid* ii. 311 (Quintilian viii. 6. 25).
[49] Terence *Eunuch* iii. 5. 64.

[50] Quintilian viii. 6. 25.
[51] Horace *Satires* ii. 5. 82.
[52] Horace *Odes* i. 4. 13 (Quintilian viii. 6. 26-27).
[53] Quintilian viii. 6. 26.
[54] Quintilian viii. 6. 26.
[55] Quintilian viii. 6. 26.

the arguments of the man. But since these are encountered everywhere I will not pursue the matter further.

CHAPTER XXIII

Method of Varying by Synecdoche

And synecdoche will be of great help to copia. It is called *intellectio,* since we understand one thing from another, as when from one we understand many, for example, what we have said above, the Roman victor in the battle; and the defeated Carthaginian, for Carthaginians. The whole from the part, as point, for sword; roof, for house; and *vice versa,* as, "mighty sea from on high"; and, "they bore a fountain and fire."[56] He said sea for wave, fountain for the part of the water. Thus Vergil. From the species, the genus, Horace: "more prone to rage than the Adriatic,"[57] for any sea; Vergil: "Acheloian draught,"[58] for any river; and this is not so aptly turned. From material, the thing made, as iron for sword; fir or pine for ship. From what precedes, what follows, as: he loosed her virginal girdle, i.e., he deflowered; he spurred his horse, i.e., he hastened. Likewise when we call bathed and oiled what we mean to be thought clean and shining. In short, when in any way one thing is understood from another: "they did live," for, they are dead. "We too did flourish," and, "we were Trojans."[59]

"And now the highest chimneys of the far farms are smoking."[60] We understand that night is imminent athough something quite different is said. Again we here infer from the sign the thing signified.

CHAPTER XXIV

Method of Varying by *Aequipollentia*

An excellent method of varying is employed through ἰσοδυναμία, i.e., equivalence. It consists in the addition, taking away, or doubling of a negative and in opposing words, as: he holds first place, he is not among the last; he failed to do nothing *(nihil non fecit);* no lack of *(non nihil)* deceit to be practiced on a man, i.e., some deceit. Moreover, by using a different word and adding or taking away negation, you will effect at once a new form of speech: he pleases, he does not dis-

---

56 Vergil *Aeneid* i. 114; xii. 119. 59 Vergil *Aeneid* ii. 324.
57 Horace *Odes* iii. 9. 23. 60 Vergil *Eclogues* i. 83.
58 Vergil *Georgics* i. 9.

please; I accept the condition, I do not reject the condition. But we will treat these and the remaining equivalents more precisely in their proper place. However, the relationship of those that are opposites of each other is variable; some are contraries, as: love, hate; angry, favoring; beautiful, ugly; some differ privatively, as: blind and seeing, dead and living, deaf and hearing, mute and talking. These characteristics are not predicated except of those things the nature of which is capable of the opposite. For a stone is neither said to be dead nor blind. Certain ones differ antithetically, as: I am willing, I am unwilling; learned, unlearned; he approves, he disapproves. The girl is ugly, she is not at all beautiful; she is by no means ugly, she is very beautiful; the man is not at all deaf, his hearing is excellent; his hearing is not too good, he is somewhat deaf; I am unable to disapprove. Concerning relatives we will speak shortly. To this class belong those that express action and passion: he received a severe wound from him, he inflicted a severe wound on him; certain things in Cicero are discussed by the learned, the learned discuss certain things in Cicero. These things will be treated elsewhere.

CHAPTER XXV

Method of Varying by Comparatives

In some comparative expressions this change is accomplished without negation by merely transposing the parts, as: he puts fame before money, he puts money after fame; he holds fame of less account than money, he holds money of more account than fame; he considers gain before honesty, he considers honesty after gain. And this copia also has its sources in contraries of the following sort: he esteems, he despises; he cares for, he neglects; he longs for, he loathes; and numberless similar ones.

CHAPTER XXVI

Method of Varying by Change of Relatives

Likewise an easy method of varying is by relative expressions, which also really belong to the class of contraries: She does not wish to be his wife; she does not wish him for a husband; he refuses to be the father-in-law of that one, he refuses that one for a son-in-law.

CHAPTER XXVII

Method of Varying by Amplification

Speech is varied by *auxesis*, i.e., by amplification, when in order to render something more effectively we put in place of an appropriate word a stronger one; as when we say of one who has been slain, that he has been slaughtered; of one who is dishonest, that he is a brigand; of one to whom something very distressing has happened, that he has died; of one afflicted with grief, that he is lifeless. In this class also belong those terms of exaggeration which I have mentioned before, when we call a cruel man, a torturer, a despoiler of churches, a criminal, a poisoner or an evil; and besides these: crime, monstrosity, pestilence, ruin; and finally, these: Atreus for a cruel person; Sardanapalus for an effeminate one. Concerning these, more in their proper place.

CHAPTER XXVIII

Method of Varying by Hyperbole

Hyperbole is also a means of variation, which some have named *superlatio*. By this lie, as Seneca says, we come to truth; for hyperbole says more than reality warrants, yet what is true is understood from the false, as: he could split the very rocks by his eloquence; to touch the sky with his finger; swifter than the wind; and swifter than the wings of lightning.[61]

CHAPTER XXIX

Method of Varying by Μείωσις, i.e., *Diminutio*

A different method of varying is by μείωσις, i.e., *diminutio*. For example: When we say of one who has struck another, that he has touched him; of one who has wounded, that he has hurt.[62] Sometimes *diminutio* has a savor of hyperbole, as: they scarcely cling to their bones;[63] shorter than a pygmy; he has less than nothing. But of these also we will treat in their proper place.

---

[61] Vergil *Aeneid* v. 319 (Quintilian viii. 6. 69).

[62] Quintilian viii. 4. 1.

[63] Vergil *Eclogues* iii. 103 (Quintilian viii. 6. 73).

CHAPTER XXX

Method of Varying by *Compositio*

Speech gains some variety from *compositio*. This generally depends on the figures asyndeton, polysyndeton: I came, I saw, I conquered.[64] Vergil:

> And roof and Lares
> And arms and Amyclean dog and Cretan quiver.[65]

Zeugma: this is when one word modifies several expressions. Moreover, it may be done in three ways, by having the verb precede, follow, or come in the middle; as: beauty withers with disease or age, (here it precedes); with either disease or age beauty withers, (here it follows); either with age beauty withers or with disease, (here it comes in the middle).[66] Likewise Cicero: "Passion overcame modesty; boldness, fear; madness, reason."[67] On the other hand: "For you are not such a one, Catiline, that shame ever restrained you from disgrace, or fear from peril, or reason from madness."[68] And sometimes the conjunction is not repeated through the series but the noun or verb is; that is called *epanalepsis*: "Does the nightly guard of the Palatine move you not at all? not at all the guards of the city? not at all the fear of the people? not at all this assembly of all good men? not at all this most splendid senate chamber? not at all the faces and features of these?"[69] Similar to this would be: Passion overcame modesty; boldness overcame fear; madness overcame reason. As through *synonymia*: boldness overcame fear, madness conquered reason, passion subdued modesty. Let us see then in how many ways the same expression can be varied by these figures: He despises gods, he despises men; gods he despises, men he despises; he despises both gods and men, both gods and men he despises; gods he despises, and men. Under this head come also the following: more patient of hunger than cold; more desirous of gain than of glory; dearer I hold no one; and no one do I hold dearer. Although these do not contribute so much of importance, nevertheless they are helpful: and for these reasons, on account of this, on this account, for a reason so slight, for so slight a reason. I shall come to you whenever the father so wishes; whenever the father so wishes I shall come to you. It is the same method when from a single

---

[64] Caesar quoted in Suetonius *Lives of the Caesars* 1. 37. 2.

[65] Vergil *Georgics* iii. 344 (Quintilian ix. 3. 51).

[66] *Rhetoric for Herennius* iv. 27. 38. somewhat modified.

[67] Cicero *For Cluentius* 6 (Quintilian ix. 3. 62).

[68] Cicero *Against Catiline* 1. 9 (Quintilian ix. 3. 62).

[69] Cicero *Against Catiline* 1. 1.

[36]

expression we make a double, or *vice versa,* as: you owe all of your possessions to me; whatever you have, you owe entirely to me.

CHAPTER XXXI

Method of Varying through Σύνταξις, i.e., *Constructio*

Some variety of speech likewise comes from syntax or proper connection, a subject that we touched upon above. For there are several expressions that admit of different constructions, as: much modesty, much of modesty; he wrote me, he wrote to me; he drank the whole night long, he drank throughout the night; most distinguished of the Romans, most distinguished among the Romans.

CHAPTER XXXII

Method of Varying through Changing the Figure in Various Ways

A speech is varied when it is presented in such a way as to alter its emotional tone and, as it were, exhibited in different attire, which may be called change of figure, as, nothing is more vain than you, or is there anything vainer than you? Here the figure is varied by use of an interrogative. The people do not care for such things, doubtless the people care for such things. Here the force of the expression is changed by use of irony. He loves money passionately; Ye gods, how he loves money! The color of the expression is changed here by use of *admiratio*. He despises both gods and men, I do not know whether he despises gods or men more. Here the form of expression is changed by use of *dubitatio*. I never thought of such things! Ye better gods, how could I have thought such things! Here the color is changed by use of *abominatio*. He is a man of unusual vanity, O the singular vanity of the man! Here through use of exclamation. Since you are of the lowest birth, no substance, no learning, no beauty, no genius, what reason do you have to boast so much? What do you have that you are so insolent? Noble birth? but you are of most obscure family. Wealth? but you are poorer than Irus. Erudition? but you have never applied yourself to good books. Beauty? but you are uglier than Thersites himself. Genius? but you were surely born stupid. What then, is your boasting but sheer insanity? Here the form of the speech is varied by *subjectio*. And in truth the oration can be varied not only by means of all figures, but also by means of nearly all the places of logic. But since these matters seem rather to pertain to copia of thought, we will treat them more fully in Book II. In this first book we have briefly pointed out nearly all forms by which speech is altered without changing the thought.

Chapter XXXIII

Practice

Now, to make the matter clearer, let us set forth an expression as an experiment and try how far it is possible to have it turn like Proteus into several forms; not that every method of varying is suitable in any one instance, but as many as are, we shall use. Let us take the following sentence for an example: *Your letter has delighted me very much.* *Your* does not admit of a synonym. Your fulness, your sublimity, your grandeur, are *periphrasis.* If you use a proper name, for instance, Faustus, it is *heterosis,* both of part of speech and of person, Faustus' letter. If Faustine letter, there is *heterosis* of the substantive in the epithet.

Letter

Epistle, letter, writing are synonyms. Little letter, little epistle, little writing constitute *heterosis.* Written sheet is synecdoche; what you have written to me, *periphrasis.*

Me

My mind, my heart, my eyes is either *periphrasis* or synecdoche; us for me is enallage of number; Erasmus is *heterosis* of person.

Very Much

Greatly, mightily, exceedingly, wonderfully, in a wonderful manner, etc. are synonyms. In the most profound manner, above measure, beyond measure, in an extraordinary degree, is *auxesis.* Not indifferently, not a little, not commonly is *contrarium* and negation. It is impossible to say how greatly, incredible to say, I cannot express in words, and others of that type savor of hyperbole.

Has Delighted

Has pleased, has refreshed, has exhilarated, are synonymous, except that there seems to be metaphor in has exhilarated. Has brought pleasure, has been a pleasure, has been a joy, etc. constitute *periphrasis.* Has imbued with joy, has been honeyed are metaphorical; has been not unpleasant, not disagreeable, substitutions of contraries.

[38]

Others cannot readily be illustrated without a context. Now then let us make trial. Your letter has delighted me very much. In a wonderful way your letter has delighted me; in an unusually wonderful way your letter has delighted me. Up to this point almost nothing has been varied except the word order. By your letter I have been greatly delighted. I have been delighted in an unusually wonderful way by your letter. Here only the voice of the verb has been changed. Your epistle has cheered me exceedingly. In truth by your epistle I have been exceedingly cheered. Your note has refreshed my spirit in no indifferent manner. By the writing of your humanity I have been refreshed in spirit in no indifferent manner. From your most pleasing letter I have had incredible joy. Your paper has been the occasion of an unusual pleasure for me. From your paper I have received a wondrous pleasure. What you wrote has brought me the deepest delight. From what you wrote the deepest joy has been brought me. From the letter of your excellency we have drunk a great joy; this is *relatio.* Anyone may easily compose others for himself. From the letter of my Faustus I have drunk the greatest joy. A by no means common joy has come to me from what you wrote. I have been uniquely delighted by your letter. I have received a wonderful delight from the letter of Faustus. How exceedingly your letter has delighted my spirit. Your paper has imbued me with ineffable delight. This is metaphor. Through your letter I have been imbued with an unusual delight. What you wrote has given me incredible pleasure. This is metaphor also. Your letter provided me with no little delight. I have been exceedingly delighted by reading your letter. The reading of your letter imbued my mind with singular joy. Your epistle was very delightful. Your letter was a source of extraordinary pleasure for me. From your letter I had a singular pleasure. You epistle was the geatest joy to me. What you wrote was the keenest delight to me. Your epistle was an incredible pleasure to me. Your epistle was immeasurably pleasing to me. You would scarcely believe how greatly I enjoy *(acquiescam)* what you wrote. Cicero frequently used *acquiescere* in this way for *oblectare.* Your epistle was the keenest enjoyment for me. Your letter has been most delightful. A singular pleasure has been provided for me by your letter. Your letter has been the occasion of glad joy for me. On receiving your letter I was carried away with joy. When your letter came I was filled with joy. On reading your most loving letter I was seized with an unusual pleasure. When I received your letter an incredible joy seized my spirit. Your epistle caressed me with extraordinary pleasure. What you wrote to me was most delightful. That you sent a letter to me was exceedingly pleasant. Nothing could have given me more pleasure than that you deemed me worthy of your letter. Your dear letter has

[39]

made me rejoice exceedingly. By your letter I am made exceedingly joyful.

That you have informed me by your letter is not only acceptable to me, but in truth delightful. You should have seen me transported by the extent of my joy when your letter reached me. That you would greet me at least by letter was certainly delightful. Nothing more longed for than your letter could have come to me. Your very anxiously awaited letter has come. Nothing more desired than your letter could have come. In these last three there is *metalepsis* or at least synecdoche; for those things which we greatly desire are customarily considered pleasing. The letter of Faustus to Erasmus is unable not to be most pleasing. Not unpleasing to me was your letter. Your by no means disagreeable letter has come to me. Your writing in no way displeasing to me has come. Your letter was as charming to me as the most charming things. I have read your letter through with great pleasure. I have received your letter not without the keenest pleasure. He who handed me your letter, brought me a heap of joys. It is wonderful to say how your letter has taken hold of me. I have received the letter you sent; it lightens my heart with a new light of joys. Whatever there was of sadness in my heart, your letter cast out straightway. I felt a wondrous joy in my heart when your letter came to me. An uncommon pleasure entered my spirit from your letter. Your letter was the cause of my abundant rejoicing. Your letter made me rejoice exceedingly. It is scarcely possible to say how much joy came to me from your letter. I can hardly express in words how much pleasure was provided me by your letter. It is wonderful to say how much joy shone upon me from your letter. Immortal God! what great joy came to us from your letter? O wonderful, what great cause of joy your letter supplied! Good gods, what a great number of joys did your writing afford me? Your letter brought me greater joy than I can express. Your letter brought me very great pleasure. You would scarcely believe what a multitude of joys your letter brought to my spirit. I am not able to say in words with what great joys your letter loaded me. Why should I fear to speak thus when Terence spoke of "the day loaded with many advantages." Your letter has made me laden with joys. I rejoiced exceedingly in your letter. I took a unique pleasure in your letter. Your writing poured forth a most rich abundance of pleasure. Your letter was most pleasurable to me. By your letter the wrinkles were straightway wiped from my brow. Directly I saw your letter, I smoothed the brow of my spirit. While I read what you wrote to me, a wonderful pleasure stole into my heart. While I looked at your letter an extraordinary multitude of joys seized my mind. When I looked at your letter an incredible wave of joy entered my heart. When I received

[40]

your most kind letter, a great joy possessed me entirely. I would die if anything more pleasing than your letter ever happened. I would perish if anything in life occurred more pleasurable than your letter. I call the muses to witness that nothing has ever before brought me more joy than your letter. Do not believe that Fortune can offer anything more pleasing than your letter. The delight your letter gives me is equalled only by the love I bear you. Oh wonderful! How much joy your letter aroused in me. What laughter, what applause, what exultant dancing your letter caused in me. Reading your most elegant letter I was touched with a strange joy. Your pen has sated me with joys. Your letter has afforded me much pleasure. Your so fine letter has wholly imbued me with joy. Your letter has imbued me with a rare pleasure. Your letter has covered my soul with an unusual pleasure. Nothing dearer than your letter has ever happened to me. I have never seen anything more joyful than your letter. There is nothing I shall receive with a gladder spirit than the next letter of my Faustus. With what joy do you suppose I am filled when I recognize your soul in your letter. When the letter carrier handed me your letter, my spirit at once began to thrill with an ineffable joy. How shall I tell you what joy titillated the spirit of your Erasmus when he received your letter. My spirit overflowed, as it were, with joy when your letter was given to me. How gladly I received your letter. After your note was brought to me, my spirit truly glowed with joy. I was almost insane with joy when I received your letter. The charm of your letter stays my spirit with extraordinary joy. I am unable to refrain from rejoicing exceedingly whenever your letters come to me. Your letter was pure honey to me. Whatever letters come from you seem to overflow with saccharin and honey. I am sumptuously refreshed by the rich banquets of your letters. Your writings are sweeter than any ambrosia. The letter of my Faustus was more sumptuous even than Sicilian feasts. There is no pleasure, no charm which I would compare with your letter. All things are sickening compared to your letter. The heart of Erasmus leaped with joy on reading your most affectionate letter. The papers covered with your writing completely filled me with joy. Whatever letter comes from you is pure joy to my heart. Your letter is alive with joy. He brought me a festal day who brought me your letter. I would have preferred what you wrote to any nectar. I would not have compared any Attic honey with your most affectionate letter. Saccharin is not sweet if it is compared with your letter. No draught of men has such a flavor as your letter has for me. What wine is to a man thirsting for it, your letter is to me. What clover is to bees, what willow boughs are to goats, what honey is to the bear, your letter is to me. The letter of your sublimity was sweeter to me than any honey. When I received

your so eagerly awaited letter, you would have said that Erasmus was
certainly drunk with joy. As soon as your letter came, you would have
seen me as though drunk with excessive joy. As utterly as I love you,
so utterly am I delighted by your letter. What you wrote seems nothing but pure charm to me. No dainty so caresses the palate as your
letter charms my spirit. No luxuries titillate the palate more agreeably
than what you wrote titillates my mind. Ἀμάξα ἡδονῶν, i.e., a wagon
full of pleasures, he brought who brought your letter. Your letter
brought me a δάθον (well) of pleasures when your letter was given to
me. He carried a θάλασσα (sea) of joys who brought your letter. To me
your letter was assuredly what Διὸς ἐγκέφαλος, i.e., brain of Zeus, was
to the Persians.

If any of these appear to be of such a sort as would scarcely be
considered suitable in prose, remember that this exercise is adapted
to the composition of verse also.[70]

[70] As explained in the Introduction
   (pp. 1-8) only the first thirty-three
   chapters of Book 1 are included in
   this translation.

ON COPIA OF THOUGHT

BOOK II

And Next Concerning the First Method of Embellishing

Now that we have stated our ideas on copia of words as briefly as
we were able, it remains for us to touch upon copia of thought briefly.
And so, to begin this part of the work with those matters that are most
nearly related to the former, the first way to embellish thought is to
relate at length and treat in detail something that could be expressed
summarily and in general. And this, in fact, is the same as if one
should display merchandise first through a latticework, or rolled up
in carpets, then should unroll the carpets and disclose the merchandise, exposing it completely to sight. An example of this method follows:

He lost everything through excess.

This expression, complete in itself, and, as it were, all rolled up,
may be developed by enumerating a great many kinds of possessions,
and by setting forth various ways of losing property. Whatever had
come by inheritance from father or mother, whatever had come by
death of other relatives, whatever had been added from his wife's
dowry, which was not at all mean, whatever had accrued from be-
quests (and considerable had accrued), whatever he had received from
the liberality of his prince, whatever private property he had procured,
all money, military equipment, clothes, estates, fields, together with
farms and herds, in short, everything, whether movable or real estate,
and finally even his immediate household property, in a short time
he so consumed, wasted, and devoured in foulest passion for harlots,
in daily banquets, in sumptuous entertainments, nightly drinking bouts,
low taverns, delicacies, perfumes, dice, and gaming that what remained
to him would not equal a farthing. In this case the words *everything*
and *he lost by excess* are developed in detail. We will add yet another:

He has finished his education.

This is a general statement. You will be able to develop this by
recounting one by one the individual disciplines—every field of learning. There is no branch of learning at all in which he has not been
elaborately trained, no discipline which he has not learned thoroughly
to the smallest detail, and has so learned that he seems to have worked
in that one alone. Further, he knows wonderfully well all the stories
of the poets; and more, he has a rich fund of the ornaments of the
rhetoricians, and has also studied the difficult canons of the gram-

[43]

marians. He is versed in the subtleties of the dialecticians; he has traced out the mysteries of natural philosophy, he has conquered the difficulties of metaphysics, he has penetrated the abstruseness of the theologians, he has learned the demonstrations of mathematics, likewise he is versed in the movements of the stars, the systems of numbers, the surveying of land, the location of cities, mountains, rivers and springs, their names and the distances between them, the harmonies and intervals of tones. Further, whatever of history there is, both ancient and modern, he knows. Whatever there is of good authors, of antiquity or of modern times, all that he has. Add to these an equal competence in Greek and Latin literature and languages; finally, whatever learning of any time has been acquired and handed down by eminent authors, all that, this man has completely comprehended and learned and holds in his mind. Another:

Endowed with all the gifts of nature and fortune.

If anyone should wish to develop this, he will relate the individual physical advantages, then one by one the gifts of intellect and of character, lastly, family, wealth, country, success and whatever good fortune commonly brings. Again, a third example will be *omniscient Hippias.* If anyone wished to expand this, he could repeat with a varied copia of words all those things that Apuleius recounts in his description of Hippias in the *Florida.*

There survives a most appropriate example of this method in Lucian, in the *Harmonides.* For although he could have summarily said, "I have learned the whole art of flute playing," he preferred to display copia by developing details in this manner. "You have taught me how to play the flute correctly, and to blow on the mouthpiece lightly, as it were, and with harmony, then, with skilled and facile touch to use my fingers in frequent raising and lowering of the tone; morever you have taught me to keep time and, furthermore, to note what is proper to any type of harmony, the divine impetus of the Phrygian, the Bacchic fury of the Lydian, the sobriety and restraint of the Doric, the cheerfulness of the Ionic, so that the modes harmonize with the dance."[1] If in the last example above the author had seen fit to do in each branch of learning what Lucian did here in the one field of music, you can see how great copia of speech there would have been.

In this connection I should not think it out of place to make this suggestion, that a general statement of the subject be placed at the beginning and that the same be then repeated in another form of speech, and that finally you should return to the general statement as though at last wearied of enumerating details, even though nothing

[1] Lucian *Harmonides* 1.

[44]

has been omitted. Moreover, we must be careful not to confuse the regular succession of details with a chaotic mass of words, and we must take care not to make everything topsy-turvy, so that we do not accumulate an unmanageable multitude of words, wholly lacking in charm, but *do* prevent the boredom of our hearer or reader by skillful arrangement, or fitting distribution, or elegant description. To this class belongs also the case where the subject may not be divided into classes but must be partitioned. For example, he is wholly a monster, will be expanded by first dividing man into body and spirit, then mentioning the individual parts of the body, likewise the individual parts of the spirit: He is a monster in body and spirit; whatever you observe in his body or spirit you will find monstrous, a shaking head, a dog's eyes, the mouth of a serpent, the features of a fury, a distended paunch of a belly, hands hooked for rapine, twisted feet—finally even the whole shape of his body. What but a monster is displayed in all these? Note that beast's tongue and voice, you will say—a monstrosity; examine his nature, you will discover a monster. Consider his character, examine his life, you will find all things monstrous, and, not to pursue details, every inch of him is nothing but monster. Here if one wanted to linger over the painting, as it were, of the details, it is amply evident how much richness might be added to the speech. Another example also:

He was drenched.

From his topmost hair to the very bottom of his shoe he was wet with rain: Head, shoulders, chest, stomach, legs, in a word, his whole body was dripping with water. It may be worthwhile to mention that this first method can also be used for the sort of expression in which we add a generalization to some more specific statement. This is done chiefly for the purpose of amplifying: While every field of knowledge contributes much to the ornament and advantage of mortals, philosophy does so especially. Likewise, license is disgusting at every age to be sure, but it is by far most disgusting in old age. Likewise, while prudence is of great importance in everything, it is especially so in wars. For the simple statement was that prudence is of great importance in wars. Of this type is that example in Cicero's oration *For His House* before the Pontifices: "While many things, Pontifices, were discovered and established by our ancestors with the help of the gods, nothing was more striking than their decision that you be at the head of the religious rites of the immortal gods and also at the head of the state."[2] Although of what consequence is it to cite this one example of this class, since they are to be met with everywhere?

2 Cicero *For His House* 1. 1.

[45]

Second Method of Varying

The second method of varying is closely related to the first. Whenever we are not content to set forth briefly the conclusion of a matter,
allowing the various things that lead up to it to be understood of
themselves, we relate them one by one. The following will serve as
an example of this precept: Cicero suppressed the undertakings of
Catiline. You will enrich this thus: The nefarious undertakings of
Catiline, who with the aid of the most abandoned young men plotted
the destruction and extermination of the whole Roman state, Marcus
Tullius Cicero, Consul, straightway suspected by his sagacity, investi-
gated with singular vigilance, apprehended with greatest good judgment, revealed with wondrous zeal for the republic, proved clearly
with incredible eloquence, put down with most weighty authority,
destroyed with arms, abolished with great good fortune.

Likewise another: He was the father of a son by this girl. You may
expand in this way: He was madly in love with this girl because she
was of singular beauty. Then impatient of love, he tempted the mind
of the simple girl with promises, enticed her with gifts, cajoled her
with flattery, seduced her into mutual love by his favors, overcame her
by wickedness, and finally had intercourse with her and deflowered
her. Some time later the womb of the girl began to swell, a child doubtless having been conceived. At length in exactly nine months she was
in labor and brought forth a boy.

Likewise another example: He took the city. This can be amplified
thus: First, Fetiales are sent to demand restitution, and also to offer
terms of peace; when the townspeople reject them, he levies troops
everywhere, accumulates a very great force of military machines, moves
the army together with the machines to the walls of the city. Those on
the other side sharply repel the enemy from the walls, but at length
he, superior in the fight, scales the walls, invades the city, and takes
possession.

Third Method

From the second method again, the third method of amplification
of speech does not differ a very great deal. In this one we do not just
set forth a bare fact, but recount also the underlying causes, the be-
ginnings from which it developed; as if it should not be sufficient for
anyone to have said that he had waged war with the Neapolitan
Gauls, but likewise he should add what the causes of hostility were,
who the instigator, what the occasion for the outbreak of the war,
what the hope of conquering, what the confidence on each side. This
precept is so clear as not to need illustration and it would be difficult
to give an example except in a great many words. Therefore we shall
omit it and refer the reader to Sallust and Livy.

Fourth Method

And now greatly varying from the above methods is the fourth method of amplification: whenever we do not relate a matter simply, but enumerate likewise the concomitant or resultant circumstances. Suppose the general statement to be: We will charge the war to your account. You will be able to expand it in this way: A treasury exhausted against barbarian soldiers, a youth broken by hardships, crops trampled underfoot, herds driven off, burned villages and farms everywhere, fields lying waste, overturned walls, looted homes, pillaged shrines, so many childless old people, so many orphaned children, so many widowed matrons, so many virgins shamefully outraged, the character of so many young people ruined by license, such great sorrow, such great grief, so many tears, and moreover, the extinction of the arts, oppressive laws, the obliteration of religion, the chaos of all things human and divine, the government of the state corrupted, this whole array of evils that arises from war, I say, we shall lay to your charge alone, since indeed you were the author of the war.

Fifth Method

The fifth method of amplification concerns ἐνέργεια which is translated *Evidentia*. We use this whenever, for the sake of amplifying, adorning, or pleasing, we do not state a thing simply, but set it forth to be viewed as though portrayed in color on a tablet, so that it may seem that we have painted, not narrated, and that the reader has seen, not read. We will be able to do this well if we first conceive a mental picture of the subject with all its attendant circumstances. Then we should so portray it in words and fitting figures that it is as clear and graphic as possible to the reader. In this sort of excellence all the poets are eminent but especially Homer, as we shall point out in the proper places. The method consists chiefly of the description of things, times, places, and persons.

DESCRIPTION OF A THING

We shall enrich speech by description of a thing when we do not relate what is done, or has been done, summarily or sketchily, but place it before the reader painted with all the colors of rhetoric, so that at length it draws the hearer or reader outside himself as in the theatre. The Greeks call this ὑποτύπωσις from painting the picture of things. This word is commonly used, likewise, for whatever is brought before the eyes. For example, to quote from Quintilian, "if someone should say that a city was captured, he doubtless comprehends in that general statement everything that attends such fortune, but if you develop what is implicit in the one word, flames will appear pouring through homes and temples; the crash of falling buildings will be heard, and

[47]

one indefinable sound of diverse outcries; some will be seen in be-
wildered flight, others clinging in the last embrace of their relatives;
there will be the wailing of infants and women, old people cruelly
preserved by fate till that day, the pillaging of profane and sacred
objects, the running about of those carrying off booty and those seeking it, prisoners in chains before their captors, and the mother struggling
to keep her infant, and fighting among the victors wherever there is
greater plunder. For although the overthrow of a city involves all these
things, it is nevertheless less effective to tell the whole at once than it
is to relate all the particulars."[3] Thus far Quintilian. Likewise as illustration of this he cites this example from Caelius' *Against Antony*:
"For they found him sunk in a drunken stupor, snoring with all his
might, repeatedly belching, while the most beautiful of his dinner
companions leaned toward him from all their various couches and the
others lay about here and there. Half-dead with fright, having learned
of the approach of the enemy, they were trying to arouse Antony. In
vain they were shouting his name and raising his head; one whispered
gently in his ear while another slapped him forcibly. But whenever
he became aware of their voice and touch, he sought to embrace the
neck of the nearest; having been aroused, he was unable to sleep, and
being too drunk, he was unable to awaken, but was thrown about in
a semiconscious sleep in the arms of his centurions and concubines."[4]
Nothing, says Quintilian, could be painted more credibly than this, nor
could any reproach be more forceful, nor anything be pictured more
clearly. He also presents a description of a luxurious banquet. "I
seemed," he said, "to see some people entering, while others were going
out, some reeling from wine, some sluggish from yesterday's drinking.
The ground was filthy, muddy with wine, covered with withered gar-
lands and the bones of fishes."[5] But there is a great abundance of this
sort of example everywhere, especially in the poets, as has been said,
and next to poets, in historians. But especially are the narratives of
messengers in tragedies remarkably rich in this excellence, because
they are presented instead of the spectacle and they report the things
which it is either impossible or inappropriate to present on the stage.
As when in Euripides' *Hecuba*, Talthybius relates to Hecuba how
Polyxena was slain; and in the *Iphigenia in Aulis* the messenger tells
how Iphigenia was killed. In the *Troades* of Seneca, the messenger re-
ports to Andromache how her son Astyanax had perished. Enough
examples have been pointed out, since all tragedies abound in narrations of this kind. Nor does it matter for this purpose whether they are
true or false, as in the *Electra* of Sophocles, the old man tells Clytem-

[3] Quintilian viii. 3. 67.   [5] Quintilian viii. 3. 66.
[4] Quintilian iv. 2. 123.

[48]

nestra falsely how Orestes had perished in battle. Also Cicero is an admirable craftsman in this technique. I think it should be pointed out that this type of description consists chiefly in an exposition of details, of those in particular that most forcefully bring a thing before one's eyes, and produce an arresting narrative, and yet *collationes,* similes, *dissimilia, imagines,* metaphors, allegories and whatever other figures illustrate the matter may be advantageously employed. Even epithets are very effective for this purpose. As when we say lofty crags, turreted cities, cerulean or glassy sea, bending ploughman, proud philosopher, spreading beech, dark chasm, and, in Homer, hateful war, and Hector with glancing helm, Ares, bane of men, and stormer of walls. The poet nowhere has any lack of this type. And in a description we do not include only what has preceded, what was contemporary with, and what followed an event, but likewise point out what did not happen or what could have happened if this or that had happened, or what can happen, as if someone should say, "See to what a crisis you have led the state, you who have rashly joined battle with the enemy." For indeed if by any chance of fortune the enemy had conquered, these things, and these would have happened. Or if someone should speak against monarchy, he would by description set before the eyes of his hearers all the tragedy of tyranny; from time to time he would admonish his audience to imagine that they actually saw all these things that would happen as soon as they changed democracy to monarchy. Furthermore, if it is a question of a serious matter, then ὑποτυπώσεις, i.e., delineations, should be employed in so far as they are profitable. But when the whole thing looks to pleasure, as is generally the case in poetry, one may indulge more freely in artifices of this sort, in ἀποδείξεις, i.e., in demonstrations, and those things that are treated for the exercise or display of genius. To this class belong the descriptions of Homer, when he arms his gods or heroes, or describes the banquet, the battle, the rout, the council. For what he does not set before the eyes by suitable details, which although they sometimes seem minute, nevertheless, I know not how, bring the thing before your eyes in a marvelous manner, he does by epithets, as well as by use of similes. Then there are descriptions of whirlwinds, of storms, or of shipwrecks, such as occur in many places in Homer, in the first book of Vergil's *Aeneid,* in the eleventh book of Ovid's *Metamorphoses;* of barbarian combat in Juvenal, of pestilence, as in the third book of Vergil's *Georgics,* in Ovid, in Seneca's *Oedipus,* and in Thucydides; and of famine, of which type there is a brilliant example in a certain declamation of Quintilian; and of portents, eclipses of the sun, and of snow, rain, rivers, thunders, earthquakes, fires, floods, which sort is Ovid's description of the flood of Deucalion; of seditions, armies,

[49]

battles, massacres, destruction, pillagings, single combat, naval warfare, such as in Lucan's third book; of a feast, banquets, weddings, funerals, triumphs, games, processions, of which kind is the description in Plutarch in his *Life of Antony* of the ship of Cleopatra; of sacred things, of ceremonies, incantations, of evil deeds as in the sixth book of Lucan. Likewise in Horace, in the *Satires,* in the role of Priapus telling what he has seen; of hunts, such as that of Cardinal Adrian, although scholars deny that the poem is his. Likewise of living things, such as the description of the electric ray and the porcupine in Claudian, and in the same author and likewise in Lactantius, of a Phoenix; of a parrot in Ovid's *Amores* and in Statius; of serpents in the ninth book of Lucan; of many fishes in Oppius; in Pliny, the description not only of numberless living things, their natures, conduct, battles, unions, but especially of a gnat; in Martial, the description of a horse and an ox, and an admirable one of bees; likewise of statues, e.g., the statute of an old man, as the one in the *Letters* of Pliny; of paintings and pictures such as that of Hercules Gallicus in Lucian; in Philostratus' various accounts of pictures; and similar accounts of woven things, and sculptures or like works of which there are innumerable examples in the poets and historians, as Arachne's web in Ovid's sixth book of the *Metamorphoses,* or the shield of Achilles, described by Homer, and of Aeneas by Vergil. Add to these, descriptions of a ship, garments, a panoply, a machine, a chariot, a colossus, a pyramid, or of any other similar things, the description of which would give pleasure. In my opinion this class should include descriptions of kinds of people and ways of life: as though one should place before your eyes a picture of the Scyths, the Androphagi, the Indians, the Troglodytes, or similar peoples. Or if you should paint a picture of the military life, the philosophic, the courtly, the rustic, the private, or the kingly. However, to express these things well, not only is art and genius necessary, but also it is of paramount importance to have actually seen what you wish to describe.

Also there are fabulous descriptions which nevertheless deal with actual things: such as descriptions of the golden age, of the silver, of the iron. Of this sort also is the picture of human life in Cebetes; of the court, of calumny, of education and several others in Lucian; of Rumor, Mischief, and the Prayers in Homer; of hunger and malice in Ovid; in the same author and likewise in Vergil, of Rumor. But if one prefers to classify these as descriptions of a person, concerning which I shall speak directly, I certainly do not greatly object.

DESCRIPTION OF A PERSON

After this comes description of persons, which is called prosopopoeia, although prosopographia or what is widely known by this name, is somewhat different from it. You might as well call those examples just mentioned concerning hunger and also envy and sleep prosopographia. For each is presented as a sort of personification. And to this class belong the figures of virtue and of pleasure that, according to Xenophon, Prodicus the Sophist represents in his *Hercules* as disputing with one another; and of death and life, that Ennius (according to Quintilian) introduces in his *Satires* as contestants. Likewise the figure of calumny, in Lucian, and in the same author, of learning, and of statuary; of opportunity, in Ausonius; of fortune, in Horace in the *Odes,* and in Q. Curtius; of greed, in Moschus; of poverty and wealth, in Aristophanes; of justice, in Chrysippus, according to Gellius; of philosophy, in Boethius; of a vampire, in Politian. Likewise of the muses, graces, furies, Bellona, the Sphinx, Scylla, Charybdis, and similar ones in the poets.

There are some closer to actuality, but yet quite suitable for display. Of this sort is the description of Hippias in Lucian and of the same person in Apuleius' *Florida;* but *notatio* is more suitable for the orator. For *notatio* is the name of these character sketches of a voluptuous lover, a miser, a glutton, a drunkard, a sluggard, a garrulous person, a braggart, a show off, an envious person, a sycophant, a parasite or a pimp. There is an example of this type in Book IV of the *Rhetoric for Herennius,* where a pseudomillionaire is depicted through his distinctive characteristics as a boaster of riches, although he was a pauper. In addition, one may take as many examples as he wishes from comedies. For comedy is concerned with nothing else. There exist, moreover, sketches useful for this purpose under the name of Theophrastus, although they seem to me to be the work of some *grammaticus* rather than of a philosopher. Hence, material for the portrait is drawn from all circumstances, but especially from these: From nationality or country, as if you should describe the appearance, culture, speech, language, bearing, gait, religious practices, temperament, and customs of a Carthaginian, Greek, Gaul, Scythian, Irishman, Spaniard, Scot, Englishman. Moreover, a Carthaginian is to be depicted as perfidious, sly, insolent, of ostentatious manner, and likewise with the others. And citizens of various countries have distinctive characteristics, as: effeminate Athenians, more versed in speech than action; austere Romans; thrifty Florentines. Such material is also drawn from sex, a man is painted as very austere, a woman very talkative, very changeable, very superstitious; from age, we depict such things as Horace points out in the *Art of Poetry;* from fortune, the wealthy man is drawn as very haughty, the poor man as very humble and timid; from disposition, the soldier is made vainglorious and immoderately boastful of his own deeds; the pimp, perjured; the rustic, too morose; the courtier, too cringing; the city man, too soft; the doctor, too anxious for gain; the poet, too eager for renown, delighting in fountains, groves, and retreats, a despiser of wealth and worldly goods; the sophist, more talkative than wise. Nor are the common affections to be overlooked: the feeling of a father for his children, a husband for his wife, a citizen for his country, a prince for his people, the people for the nobility, and others which Aristotle recounts in great detail in his *Rhetoric.* Moreover, there are also peculiar differences in each of these. It is not enough to understand what is appropriate to an old man, a youth, a slave, the father of a family, a pimp; otherwise the individuals in these classes would always be treated without individuality. The comic poets especially appear to have aimed at variety in persons of the same class. For how could two people be more dissimilar than Demea and Mitio in Terence; when the latter rebukes his son most severely, the former is pleasant; when the latter is especially pleasant, the former is severe. And yet each is an old man, and to that extent brothers. Who could be more different than Chremes, always calm and civil, and Simo, vehement and suspicious or, likewise, than prudent Pamphilius, and Charinus, destitute of spirit and wisdom? Who so unlike as Phaedria fighting vice, and Chaerea completely without scruples? Likewise, is there anything in common between Davus, most pertinacious author of hope, and Byrria, messenger of nothing but desperation? Or very much between Gnathas and Phormio? And the parasites of Plautus are far different from either one, just as the prostitutes of the latter also differ greatly from those of Terence. Terence depicts courtesans almost as good women—for example, Philotis and Bacchides in the *Hecyra;* Plautus, old men as loving and jovial, and cunning deceivers of their wives, although he makes Euclio extremely obstinate and suspicious of other women.

But if we treat a character used by another, the proper treatment is to be sought from those who depicted or described them before; for example, if you should treat Achilles you ought to depict him as impetuous, inexorable, frank, a foe of kings, a foe of the mendacious, swift of foot, for Homer painted him first thus; Ulysses, on the contrary, you ought to depict as crafty, deceptive, dissimulating, tolerant of everything; Agamemnon, less hard in spirit, but greedy for power, fearful of the people, more desirous of pleasure than war; Hector, sublime of spirit, careless of death and auguries, esteeming his fatherland above all things; Ajax, more prompt in deed than speech, impatient of abuse and denial. In short, as Homer has depicted the character of anyone, so ought the tragic poets to represent that person. Likewise, if anyone should desire to depict Aristotle, Themistocles,

[52]

Phocion, Alcibiades, Pisistratus, Julius Caesar, Fabius or Camillus, or Timo, Socrates, Plato, or Epicurus, the proper treatment should be sought from the historians. This kind of exercise seems to have been approved by those who wrote the orations and epistles of Menelaus, Phaenix, Achilles, Phalaris, Brutus, Seneca and Paul. In the same way the writer of dialogue should be careful to what characters he attributes what speech. But what is proper in fictitious characters (for example, you should represent Philosophy as of sober countenance and full of authority; the Muses, simple and charming; the Graces, holding hands, and with flowing garments; Justice, upright and with steadfast glance; and others similarly) ought to be taken from the nature of the things in question. There is also a treatment proper to fables, which no one will rightly preserve unless he knows and has considered the natures of animals, so that he knows the elephant is docile and conscientious; the dolphin, an enemy of the crocodile, a friend of man; that the eagle builds his nest in high places; the beetle customarily pushes about the muck in which he gives birth and is born, and is not seen in seasons when eagles brood; the crested lark lays its eggs in grain fields; the hedgehog enjoys conversation, and is an enemy of snakes. And these things and others more recondite are easily found in Aristotle, Pliny, and Aelian. And this type is treated even by orators. But fables which attribute speech to inanimate things such as trees or rocks, seem rather forced. Prosopographies more characteristic of orators are those in which a certain character is depicted in his own colors, as it were, and to the extent which is necessary for the purpose, as in Sallust, Catilina; in Livy, Hannibal; in Plutarch, Trajan. *Effictiones,* i.e., descriptions of personal appearance, are employed sometimes, but less frequently. To this class belongs any detailed description of a beautiful woman, or on the other hand, of an ugly old woman. As Homer described Thersites, and Helen, at the request of Priam, points out from the walls many of the Greek chieftains; and Vergil, imitating him, in Book VI describes several Romans. To this class especially belongs the figure διαλογισμός, that is, *sermocinatio,* the attribution to an individual of language in harmony with his age, birth, country, life, purpose, spirit, and behavior. It is all right to compose speeches of this sort in history, for example; wherefore so many of the speeches of Thucydides, Sallust, Livy are composed, as well as letters and apophthegms, and, indeed, thoughts, as of the man talking with himself, although this is more common in the poets. It is properly called prosopopoeia whenever, with due regard to propriety, we present the character of a man far away, or long since dead, speaking. For example: what if we should now bring back to life the ancient noblemen of this city and they saw the morals of this generation, would they

[53]

not burst out in these words? Then the speech would follow. What if that ancestor of yours were here now, would he not rebuke you deservedly with these words? What if Camillus should return to life, would he not rightly exhort us with these words? And now I seem to hear him talking to me thus. And imagine Plato himself expostulating with you in this way. Less extravagant are prosopopeia of the kind that represent people as saying those things which it is probable they would say if they were present. The figure is more strained (but nevertheless acceptable in serious orations as well as in exercises, if ever the seriousness of affairs should require it) when we represent nature or the state or the province or the fatherland as speaking. As does Cicero in his speech against Catiline: "What things and in what manner does it (the Fatherland) silently say to you Catiline?" again: "For if our country, which is far dearer to me than life, if all Italy, if the whole state, should speak thus, 'Marcus Tullius what are you doing?' "[6] Socrates in Plato's *Critias* portrays the laws as arguing with him. It is a figure of this type whenever we attribute speech to the gods themselves, or to places, or to other things without speech. But those which are properly called prosopographia are made more effective by metaphors, similes and *collationes*. Among the poets there are a great number of these.

DESCRIPTION OF PLACE

Speech is enriched also by descriptions of places; the Greeks call these τοπογραφία. Frequently they are used as an introduction to narrations not only by poets, but also by historians, and sometimes by orators. It is an example of this type whenever the whole appearance of a place is portrayed just as if it were in sight, as for example, the appearance of a city, a mountain, a region, a river, a port, a villa, gardens, an amphitheatre, a fountain, a cavern, a temple, a grove. And if these descriptions are of actual places they are to be called *topographia*, but if fictional, *topothesia*. Examples of the former are the description of the Laurentine villa in Pliny's *Letters*, in Statius of the Surrentine villa of Pollius and the Tiburtine villa of Manlius. Of the latter, the abode of sleep in Ovid, the home of Rumor and the palace of the sun; of the Lower Regions and the home of Cacus in Vergil; the home of Tenarus in Statius: the house in Lucian, palace of Psyche in Apuleius. To the former type should be referred, I think, the burning of Mt. Vesuvius described by Pliny the younger; of burning Aetna in Claudian; then any description of the Nile, or the cave of Sibyl, the rainbow and other things of that sort. The more unusual these things are the more pleasure

[6] Cicero *Against Catiline* 1. 7. 18 and
   1. 11. 27 (Quintilian ix. 2. 32).

they give, and one may linger longer over them, provided only that they are not wholly strange.

DESCRIPTION OF TIME

Further, we call a description of time χρονογραφία. And not infrequently this is used as a beginning. Sometimes it is employed simply for the sake of giving pleasure, for example, as the poets describe the day, the night, the dawn or the dusk, although even then another purpose ought not to be completely lacking. An example is the one in Vergil:

> It was night, when the stars turn
> In mid-flight, when every field lies still;
> And tired bodies over the earth
> Were enjoying peaceful sleep; the woods
> And wild seas were still,
> The beasts and varicolored birds, those that far
> And wide haunt the limpid lakes, and fields rough
> With brambles, lay in sleep under the silent night,
> Healed their cares, and hearts forgot their toil.[7]

For this description of nocturnal quiet tends to emphasize the grief of Dido who was not resting even then when all things else were resting. For immediately follows:

> But not the distressed Phoenician queen, not
> Ever was she lulled in sleep.

Descriptions of spring, winter, autumn, summer, the harvest, a holiday, the Saturnalia are of this type and they are often effective for demonstration. They are used in combination whenever we discuss the state of the times, for example, of peace, of war, of sedition, of faction, of monarchy, of democracy, when we show what virtues or vices especially would flourish then. These kinds of amplification, indeed, it is sometimes suitable for the student to compose separately as an exercise; but a complete description involves all of them. Horace, in that satire which I have just cited, for example, describes first the place, the Esquiline Hill, then the time, then the characters of Priapus and the wicked women; finally he vividly pictures the sacrifice and noisy flight of the frightened victims.

Egressio, Sixth Method of Amplifying

The sixth method of amplification connected with those above, which the Greeks call παρέκβασις, some of the Romans call *egressio;* others, *digressio;* and some, *excursus.* It is, by the definition of Quintilian, a discussion departing from the main subject but still pertinent

[7] Vergil *Aeneid* iv. 522 *seq.*

and useful to the case; and it is used either to praise, for example, that famous recital of the virtues of Gnaius Pompey in Cicero's *For L. Cornelius* in which that divine orator (for I shall use the words of Quintilian) digresses abruptly from the speech he had begun, as if the thread of the speech were broken off by the mere mention of the name of the general, or to censure, or for adornment, or to charm, or to prepare for something that follows.[8] Digressions may be taken, moreover, for the most part from the same places that we have just considered. From the recounting of deeds, from the description of localities, countries, persons; likewise from the treatment of tales, fables; also from commonplaces whenever for the purpose of amplification we speak against pride, luxury, licentiousness, avarice, infamous passion, tyranny, anger and the rest of the vices, and spend time on these as though the main subject had been dropped for a time, or on the other hand, when we praise frugality, generosity, continence, the study of letters, piety and keeping silent. Those are of so much importance in speaking fluently that several famous authors have written about them; they call them χρείαι. And there are those commonplaces not unlike the above, when we contrast the advantages of freedom with the disadvantages of slavery, the mutability of fortune with the universal inevitableness of death, the great power of money in the affairs of mortals with the brevity of human life, and innumerable similar ones. Furthermore, it is permitted to delay longer in digression either at the beginning of a speech, as for instance, the description of Hercules Gallicus in Lucian, and of the Lamiae in Politian; or at the end, at which point the now tired hearer may be refreshed; Vergil does this commonly in the *Georgics*. In the middle, if it is ever proper to digress, a quick return should be made to that point whence the digression occurred, unless the part of the speech already completed offers occasion for a digression, as after the narration, where the hearer may be rendered more eager for the argument that follows, or after the proof, or in general after uninteresting places where the weariness brought on by subtlety may be dispelled; or unless the matter itself freely offers an opportunity of this sort that invites to longer delay.

Seventh Method

The seventh method of amplification is taken from epithets. Diomedes made an epithet a species of *antonomasia* and defined it as a distinguishing word placed in front of a proper name for purposes of praise, attack, or information: For purposes of praise, as, divine Camilla; of attack, as, Ulysses, author of wicked deeds; of information,

[8] Quintilian iv. 3. 13-4.

as, Larissaean Achilles. Epithets are taken from the mental powers, as, Plato, wisest of philosophers; from the body, Thersites, most deformed of all Greeks; from external goods, and that not in a general way but from all the different kinds of advantage that spring from fortune; from descent, as, noblest Maecenas; from wealth, as, Croesus, wealthiest of kings; from appearance, Nireus, most beautiful; from bodily strength, Milo, strongest of athletes; from one's country, Ulysses, the Ithacan; from achievement, Hercules, conqueror of monsters; from past events, twice captured Phrygians; in short from all the goods or troubles of fortune. Nor does it matter whether epithets are adjectival terms or not, provided only a certain characteristic be attributed in some way, not only to persons, but in truth even to things, as: headlong youth; headlong and mad counsellor, love; passion, food of evil men; sullen and difficult old age; philosophy, expeller of vices; comedy, mirror of human life; history, teacher of life. In poems it is permitted to use natural epithets, as: shining white snow, flowing fountains, freezing night, winding stream, golden sun. In prose they ought not to be employed unless they have a certain emphasis and affect the main point, as: you will not gain such an unjust request from Aristides, the most just; do you dare celebrate the Floralia before Cato, the most severe censor of morals? This is done chiefly in citations of examples or *sententiae*: Aristarchus, most learned and likewise most diligent; Cicero, prince of eloquence; Plato, most trustworthy author.

Eighth Method

The eighth method of enlarging is taken from circumstances, which the Greeks call περιστάσεις. These have to do partly with things: cause, place, occasion, instrument, time, mode and so on; partly with persons, as: race, country, sex, age, education, culture, physical appearance, fortune, position, quality of mind, desire, experiences, temperament, understanding and name. Timely and appropriate use of circumstances, moreover, has many advantages: First in amplifying and disparaging, about which we will speak briefly soon; then in vivid presentation, about which we spoke just above; and in addition, in confirmation and credibility. For it results in the whole speech being sown and fortified everywhere with close and frequent arguments, which although you do not develop, you lead forth, as it were, to the battle line; but they fight of themselves and help the cause not a little, so that, as it is possible for one, although he works in another field, to recognize, nevertheless, a man skilled in wrestling or music, so you can discern a rhetor anywhere from his skillful combining of this kind. Because they are spread throughout the whole speech, the method cannot be illustrated in a brief example.

[57]

Ninth Method of Enlarging

The ninth method of enlarging is by amplification. Several forms of this are considered by Quintilian. We shall touch briefly on those that are related to our present purpose. The first method of amplification is by *incrementum,* when by several steps not only is a climax reached, but sometimes, in some way, a point beyond the climax. There is an example of this in Cicero's fifth speech against Verres: "It is an offense to fetter a Roman citizen, a crime to flog him, treason to kill him, what shall I say it is to crucify him"[9]—there is no possible expression fully suitable to so wicked a deed. To this class belongs also that case in which, with circumstances accumulated in a regular order, something increasingly important continuously follows in the context and course (of the speech). An example of this is in Cicero's second *Philippic* about the vomiting of Antony: "O action not only disgusting to see, but also to hear. If this had happened to you at table during those monstrous drinking bouts of yours, who would not term it disgraceful? But actually in an assembly of the Roman people, the Master of the Horse, engaged in public business, for whom it would be disgraceful to belch, covered his chest and the whole tribunal with scraps of food smelling of wine."[10] Here single words carry the figure, for to vomit would have been loathsome in itself even if not in an assembly, even not an assembly of citizens, even not Romans, or even if he were not engaged in business, even if not public business, or even if he were not Master of Horse. If anyone should separate these and spend more time on the individual steps, he will certainly increase the copia of the speech, but yet he will amplify less effectively. The opposite of this is *comparatio.* For as *incrementum* looks to something higher, so *comparatio* seeks to rise from something lesser. Moreover, *comparatio* employs either a hypothetical or actual *exemplum.* An illustration of the hypothetical kind occurs in the first part of the example just quoted from Cicero. For he imagines this to have happened at table in private. There is also an example in the speech of the same orator against Catiline: "By Hercules, if my servants feared me the way all your fellow citizens fear you, I would think I ought to leave my house."[11] When using an actual *exemplum* we make the matter we are amplifying seem nearly as great or equal to or even greater than it. For example, Cicero in the *For Cluentius,* when he had related how a certain Milesian woman had taken a bribe from the alternate heirs to cause an abortion said: "Of how much greater punishment is Oppian deserving for the same injury. Since, indeed, she had attacked with vio-

[9] Cicero *Against Verres* 5. 56 (Quintilian viii. 4. 4).
[10] Cicero *Philippics* 2. 25. 63 (Quintilian viii. 4. 8. and 10).
[11] Cicero *Against Catiline* 1. 7. 17 (Quintilian viii. 4. 10).

[58]

lence her own body and harmed only herself; the latter, however, in committing the same offense harmed another."[12] In this type not only are parts compared with wholes, but also with parts, as in this passage from Cicero's first speech against Catiline: "Or in truth shall Scipio, that distinguished man, although a private citizen, have killed Tiberius Gracchus who was only slightly disturbing the State, and shall we who are consuls tolerate Catiline, who desires to lay waste the whole world with fire and slaughter?"[13] Here Catiline is compared to Gracchus, the situation of the State, to the whole world; a slight disturbance, to slaughter, fire, and laying waste; and a private citizen, to consuls. And if anyone should wish to, he can develop these fully through the use of details. And we amplify by *ratiocinatio*, when the one grows and the other is increased, in this way: "You, with that throat, that chest, that body with the strength of a gladiator, drank so much wine at the wedding of Hyppia that yesterday you had to vomit before the eyes of the Roman people."[14] Actually how great a quantity of wine Antony drank is inferred from the fact that his body with the strength of a gladiator was not able to endure or digest it. Under this heading should be classified those examples in which we raise the most hateful things to a peak of envy; we elevate them advisedly so that what is to follow may seem so much more grave. There is an example of this in Cicero: "The captain of a ship from a most noble city bought exemption from the terror of the scourge at a price. What humanity!"[15] Some extraordinarily hateful thing must be expected of him to whom these things which are atrocities seem humane and usual by comparison. And we amplify by heaping up of words and likewise of significant *sententiae*, which method is close to the figure συναθροισμός, i.e., ac-cumulatio, which was discussed above. Cicero uses this in his speech *For Ligarius*: "For what was that bared sword of yours doing on the battle front at Pharsalus, Tubero? Whose breast was that point seeking? What was the purpose of your arms? Upon what were your mind, your eyes, your hands, your bold spirit fixed? What did you desire? What were you hoping for?"[16] Here the speech was enlarged as though by a heaping up. The same result is accomplished, however, by a series of words rising higher and higher in meaning, as in this example: "There was the jailer, the executioner of the praetor, the death and terror of the allies and the Roman citizens, the lictor Sextius."[17] We

[12] Cicero *For Cluentius* 11. 32 (Quintilian viii. 4. 11).

[13] Cicero *Against Catiline* 1. 1. 3 (Quintilian viii. 4. 13).

[14] Cicero *Philippics* 2. 25. 63 (Quintilian viii. 4. 16).

[15] Cicero *Against Verres* 5. 44. 177 (Quintilian viii. 4. 19).

[16] Cicero *For Ligarius* 3. 9 (Quintilian viii. 4. 27).

[17] Cicero *Against Verres* 2. 14. 118 (Quintilian viii. 4. 27).

amplify also by a device similar to the figure *correctio,* as in Cicero *Against Verres:* "For we have brought to your judgment not a thief, but a brigand; not an adulterer, but a violator of chastity; not an impious person, but an enemy of sacred and religious things; not an assassin, but a most cruel murderer of our fellow citizens and allies."[18]

Moreover, there are as many methods of attenuating as there are of amplifying. And common methods of amplification by adverbs, nouns, or other suitable parts of speech, used either in praise or attack, pertain to copia of speech: Cicero pleases me very greatly. How kindly your father-in-law behaves to you cannot be expressed in words. I should be unable to put into words how much Cicero pleases me. But we have discussed these methods of expansion in the first book.

And that method of amplifying is known and familiar in which we magnify a species contrasted with a class, as, while all the liberal disciplines gain a great deal of distinction or advantage for a man, above all does eloquence; but we touched upon this method also above.

Tenth Method of Amplifying

The tenth method of amplifying is based on our devising the greatest possible number of propositions, i.e., rhetorical propositions, for the proof of which arguments must be offered. Now Quintilian denies that a method of devising propositions can be comprehended in a formal theory, but says that this faculty depends on natural talents and practice. And therefore it happens that although several orators who have studied the same rules will use similar types of argument, yet one devises them in greater abundance than another.[19] Propositions are taken partly from those which are common to all cases and partly from those peculiar to the case in hand. An example would be this, which Quintilian liked: When Alexander destroyed Thebes he found tablets on which it was recorded that the Thebans had loaned the Thessalians one hundred talents. These tablets he gave to the Thessalians because they had been his allies in the campaign. Afterward, when they had been restored to their city by Cassander, the Thebans demanded repayment from the Thessalians. The case is tried before the Amphictyonic council. It is admitted that the Thebans had loaned the hundred talents and had not recovered them. The whole case depends on the fact that Alexander is alleged to have given the tablets to the Thessalians. It is also admitted that the money of the Thebans was not given to the Thessalians by Alexander. In this argument, then, propositions of this sort and their supporting arguments must be devised. The first part will be, that Alexander had done nothing by

[18] Cicero *Against Verres* 5. 66. 70   [19] Quintilian v. 10. 109.
  (Quintilian viii. 4. 27).

[60]

giving; the second, he had not the power to give; the third, he had not given. And the first proposition of the first part assuredly will be in favor of the Thebans: It is permitted to seek to recover by law what has been taken away by violence. It will be in favor of the Thessalians that the tablets were not simply taken by ordinary violence, but in war. However, the *jus belli* is most powerful in human affairs; kingdoms, peoples, the boundaries of nations and cities are controlled by it. To this again the Thebans oppose another proposition, that not all things come into the power of the victor by right of war, but that for those things that can be brought before a court of justice, the right of war avails nothing; and, what has been seized by force of arms cannot be retained except by force of arms. And so where the *jus belli* has force, there is no judge; where there is a judge, the *jus belli* has no force. And this proposition, to be sure, arises out of those circumstances of the case which distinguish it from other cases. However, a similar example depends on commonplaces for proving this proposition: Prisoners of war are free when they return to their native land, because what has been won in war cannot be retained except by the same force by which it was acquired. A third proposition for the Thebans will be taken from the details peculiar to the case: It is of the utmost importance that equity be observed in this case, since it is being tried before the Amphictyonic council. For different methods are used in pleading before the centumviral court and before a private judge, even in the same cases. And so these things also are effective in making it appear that this case differs from others, in which the right of war ought to prevail. Further, a proposition of the second part for the Thebans would be: Right could not have been conferred by the victor, because only that belongs to the victor which he holds, and right, being incorporeal, cannot be held in the hand. Again, in support of this an argument from *dissimile* is offered: The position of an heir is one thing; that of a victor another. To the former passes right; to the latter, property. Moreover, another proposition complementary to the above may be drawn from the peculiar details of the case: Although we may grant that right with respect to other things passes to the victor, surely the right of public debt can in no way have passed to him, because whatever a people loan is owing to them all, and as long as one of them survives, he is creditor for the whole sum. But the Thebans had not all been in Alexander's power; and this indeed does not need proofs. A common proposition (i.e., one adaptable to any case) of the third part will be of this sort: Alexander did not give when he gave the tablets, for right does not reside in tablets; and this proposition can be defended by many arguments. From simile: For no one has tablets of inheritance, but everyone has the right to in-

[61]

herit. And if by chance a creditor lost the tablets, the debtor would not in consequence be freed of his debt. Another proposition is conjectural: Alexander's purpose in giving the Thessalians the tablets was not to honor them, but to trick them. And this ought to be supported by various inferences. The third proposition does not properly belong to this stage, but is like the beginning of a new controversy; however, it is taken from details peculiar to the subject and is of this nature: Although we grant the Thessalians everything, that the right of war has force in judgments both before these judges and in a matter of public debt, and likewise for the rest, nevertheless, if the Thebans lost anything by the conquest of Alexander, they ought to recover it through the restoration by Cassander, especially since Cassander wishes it.[20]

In the same way anyone urging Cicero not to accept the condition offered by Antony, namely that he might live if he burned his *Philippics*, could use these propositions: The preservation of life is not of such importance to any eminent man that he would give up immortal fame. A particular proposition drawn from the circumstances of the case depends on this general one: This should be especially true of Cicero who by his great exertion won for himself a most distinguished and always triumphant name and demonstrated in the many brilliant volumes which he published in great abundance that death should be scorned, and particularly since now as an old man not much of life appeared left for him. Again another major proposition will be taken from the circumstances of the case: Nothing is more unfortunate than for Cicero, the best of men, to owe his life to Antony, the worst of men. A third will be conjectural: That Antony's action is calculated, so that when the *Philippics*, on which he knows both his own eternal infamy and the everlasting glory of Cicero depend, have been burned, by taking Cicero's life he will blot out Cicero completely. Likewise, if you are dissuading any one from matrimony, you may use these propositions: First, if you consider piety, marriage is an obstacle for those hastening to Christ. Second, from the point of view of pleasure in life, an unhappy marriage brings with it innumerable vexations; and in this connection a broad field of comparison is immediately opened up between the advantages of celibacy and the disadvantages of marriage. Third, if freedom is a consideration, and how many place that even before life, the bond of marriage takes that away especially. Then you will come to particular propositions, which can be innumerable, as: You ought not to marry her, not at this time. Or, marriage is not for you, a pauper, an old man, a scholar, a valetudinarian (as the

20 Quintilian v. 10. 111 *seq.*

case may be). Moreover, we may increase the number of propositions by the use of *fictio,* as Cicero does in the *For Milo*: Suppose that Clodius was treacherously killed by Milo, nevertheless, one who would at the risk of his own head do away with a citizen so destructive of the safety of the Republic, would appear worthy of the highest honors. Then he adds in seriousness: But he did not kill him.

Likewise, the number grows when, to prepare the way ahead, we premise, in addition to the proposition under discussion, some more difficult proposition so that the one we are trying to prove will seem less difficult by contrast with it. For example, one in consultation, eager to dissuade the Roman pontiff from an attack on the Venetians, according to the proverb which says, you must ask for what is exorbitant to get what is fair, would undermine opposition in advance, thus: There are authors, by no means to be scorned, who think that dominion and temporal authority are in no way consistent with the dignity of the supreme pontiff, the peace of the church or Christian piety, which alone, disregarding everything, he ought to consult. And this proposition, one would be able to prove readily with an abundance of arguments. Then he will come to the second, in this way: These things and many similar things another would say perhaps; in truth, we may grant that there is consistency on these points, yet it is very inconsistent with the clemency of one acting in the place of Christ, who said, "Learn from me, because I am meek and humble of heart," to seek and seek again for this kind of dominion by arms, insurrection, slaughter, and blood. Then one will come to the third: Granted that it may be in the highest degree right, yet it is unsafe, because the outcome of war is uncertain; whence there is danger lest, while he is attempting to restore the condition of the church by temporal and uncertain means, he overturn it completely. And this also can be supported by many examples and similes. Then he digresses in connection with the third in this way: Granted that it may be fitting, permissible, and that you may conquer, yet such a flood of evils follows even a just war that not even a temporal ruler, if he is a Christian, ought to attack countries or cities with the sword, much less he who bears the title of Most Holy. Also there can be added this proposition from personal circumstances: That it might be fitting for another pontiff, but yet it is not so for Julius, if he be that Julius whose kind spirit and singular sanctity of life appear to abhor war. And after one has proved these things by arguments, then he will proceed to particular considerations in this way: Even though none of these things that we have related would deter us, yet at present it seems ill-advised to undertake war with the Venetians. And this proposition, which depends on circumstances, can be divided further: First, because this

[63]

war could not be undertaken without the greatest peril to Christianity; then because the Roman see, where the highest rewards have always been for pious deeds, will appear too little mindful of the dutiful acts which the successors of St. Peter often and with the greatest risk of life performed for the sake of Christianity; and finally, because there is no adequate cause for waging war against people not deserving it. Some might prefer to call these reasons rather than propositions, although nothing prevents the same expression from being both a proposition and a reason. Likewise, if anyone desired to persuade a king not to undertake a war with the most Christian king of the Gauls, he could fortify his approach to the case with these propositions: First, to engage in war is not the part of man, born to benevolence, but of brute animals to whom nature is seen to have given certain arms. This is general. The second proposition depends on it: This is not even true of all animals, but only of wild ones. On this again the third depends: And not even wild animals fight with one another in this way to the same degree as men do. For the tiger does not wage war with the tiger, nor the lion with the lion; however, man does not direct his violence against a different animal (as do the animals) but against men. Then, wild animals do not fight except to protect their young, or when driven to madness by hunger. Foolish ambition and I know not what light and affected pretexts arouse man to such bloody wars. After this, now, as a sort of new stage follows the fourth, taken from circumstances: Although some men do fight, they are barbarians not altogether different from wild animals; fighting is not for those who live by law. Add a fifth: That even if they do not engage in it, yet it is by no means the part of Christians, since indeed the Christian religion is nothing else but peace. One may add a sixth: Even if it is fitting, yet it is not expedient to undertake war, because all things considered, by far more disadvantages are incurred for the sake of war than advantages gained, even by the victor. That will then have to be developed by argument. Also a seventh will be found: Even if it is expedient, yet it is not safe; the outcome of war is uncertain. For victory is not always theirs whose cause is better, or who have the best equipment; troops sometimes even turn their arms against their own leader. But these propositions are general ones for the most part. Then one may come to particular ones, which are taken from very closely related circumstances: Although everything else is disregarded, you should not wage war, especially with such a person. And this can be divided into many: Either because you are a boy and unskilled in war, or a new king. And likewise with the rest, for I am only giving examples of the reasons. Again: War should not be waged with this king, so powerful, so deserving of good from your father, bound to

[64]

you by such close ties, so ready to serve even yourself, or, not on this pretext, not at this time, not with these troops. In the same way, if one is persuading someone not to study Greek literature, he will first essay this proposition: That none of this literature has much to do with Christian happiness, and even stands in the way of it. When he has proved this to be probable by arguments, then he continues with the subject in this way: Although we grant there is reason to devote time to other literature, certainly Greek literature should be avoided, either because it is so difficult that the life of mortals in any case fleeting, brief, and ephemeral, does not suffice to learn it, or if man's life should indeed be long enough, its study is not fruitful enough to compensate for the expenditure of even slight exertions on it. Finally: The fortune of overthrown and oppressed Greece, by a kind of fate attends those who have devoted themselves to literature of this kind. Or, even if it should be studied by others, it should not be studied by him. And now many propositions of the kind that depends on circumstances can be taken up. In propositions of this sort, I think care should be taken to arrange them as far as possible so that we can descend easily as if by steps from each one to the next. In this matter, indeed, Lucian is skillful, for example in the *Tyrannicide*, which we have made Latin: If I had only attempted so excellent a deed, at such great risk of life, I would even for that be worthy of reward. Then from this point he proceeded: Yet I not only attempted, but indeed I threw back the guards and killed the son. Shall I not bear away the rewards? Here digressing again: But I got rid of the father too, because I gave him the motive for his death. Likewise, in the *Disowned*, which we also have made Latin: It is not permitted to disown one whom you have once disowned and then taken back into the family again. Then: Even if it is indeed permitted, yet in this particular case, it is not permitted. Finally: Even if the cause be wholly sufficient, yet such is the magnitude of his former services, that for this reason the father should overlook his son's faults. But if we dislike a great number of propositions, we can comprehend a whole case in three or four. And then in treating each one, if it seems best we divide it into other propositions. The main points we sometimes set forth in the *divisio*. I call *divisio* the threshold of the argument as it were, where we explain briefly, in what order we are going to say what. Sometimes in the actual treatment of the case we proceed from one point to another, as if by steps, although if they are too dissimilar in nature, we connect them suitably with appropriate transitions like those found in this work. One striving for copia should take especial care to find those propositions that comprehend the case fully, whatever it is about, then to divide them properly, and finally to arrange them in an order as suitable to the case as possible. Of course it must be done in such a way that the speech is not confused with the copia of thought, and the hearer is certain throughout where to direct his attention, what he should remember, and what to expect. Then the speaker should not hesitate at any point where it is obvious whither he takes his way. But, as I have said, Quintilian denies that the invention of propositions can be expounded in a textbook, although this, nevertheless, is both very important and very difficult. However, natural ability will be of great help because it is of especial value in everything. Then jurisprudence is of value especially in forensic oratory; and a knowledge of moral philosophy, history, and a great many authors is useful in persuasive and demonstrative oratory. Finally, wide experience, training, and imitation are profitable. For from similar things comparisons or even contrasts are collected. Although general propositions can be devised according to the nature of the case, specific ones must come from a diligent consideration of the circumstances of the case. Then the precepts of the rhetors will aid the productive talent in handling the *heads* of cases, what Quintilian calls *status,* the Greeks στάσις. Further, the persuasive type has its own peculiar places whence it is permitted to seek propositions, the right, praiseworthy, useful, safe, easy, necessary. The demonstrative likewise has its own—namely the classes of goods and what is included in these.

The Eleventh Method

The eleventh method of enriching depends on the copious accumulation of proofs and arguments which the Greeks call πίστεις. Various reasons are employed to support the same proposition, and the reasons are confirmed by varied arguments. Some proofs, moreover, are technical, ἔντεχνοι, i.e., "artificial"; some are nontechnical, ἄτεχνοι, i.e., not connected with art. Arguments of the latter kind are derived chiefly from precedents, from rumors, from evidence taken under torture, from documents, from an oath, from witnesses. Those of the former class are taken chiefly from those signs which are closely related to the nontechnical ones: Some of these require a certain conclusion and they are called τεκμήρια; others are not of this nature and are called σημεία; then some are taken from arguments (for Quintilian distinguishes these from signs), some of which are credible, others highly probable, others not inconsistent. For the most part these are derived from circumstances, which are indeed twofold in nature, pertaining to persons or things. The personal are entirely of this sort: Family, race, country, sex, age, education, physical appearance, fortune, rank, natural disposition, desires, inclinations, previous acts and sayings, passion, wisdom, name. Circumstance of things are these: Cause, place, time, occasion, antecedents of the affair, collateral circumstances, consequences, opportunity, instrument, method.

COMMONPLACES

There are, likewise, places common to general classes and also to all divisions of cases. For the above, even if they are drawn from other places, yet are very appropriate for judicial controversies, especially the conjectural kind. Moreover, arguments are in general derived from definition, from description, from etymology, which is a kind or species of definition, from those things that pertain to the nature of definition: class, species, peculiarity, differences, partition, division, whose forms are various; from the origin, the chief point, the development; from the introduction of similes and *dissimilia;* from contraries, contradictions, consequences; from relatives, causes, events; from comparison, which is threefold, the greater, the lesser, the equal; from derived forms and whatever others there are. There is not much agreement among writers about regular order, rhythm, or words. Aristotle and Boethius have written about them at length; Cicero, accurately enough but somewhat obscurely; and Quintilian most briefly. Whoever trains himself for eloquence ought to examine individual places and go over them in detail to see what he can elicit from them. Practice will result in their suggesting themselves automatically in a never ending series. Likewise, arguments can be based on supposition, which is common to many places, and also on the details peculiar to a case.

However, most powerful for proof, and therefore for copia, is the force of *exempla*, which the Greeks call παραδείγματα. These are employed either as similes, or *dissimilia*, or contraries; also, in comparing the greater to the lesser, the lesser to the greater, or equals to equals. Dissimilarity and inequality are in class, measure, time, place, and most of the other circumstances that we have enumerated above. This class embraces the *fabula*, the apologue, the proverb, judgments, the parable, or *collatio*, the *imago* and analogy, and other similar ones. And indeed most of these are customarily used not only for producing belief but also for embellishing and illustrating, for enriching and amplifying subject matter. Therefore, if anyone is willing to collect a great number of ornaments of speech from his reading he can produce an oration as copious as he wishes; and yet it will not be a lifeless mass of words, and through its variety will avoid tedious monotony. It is not within the scope of this work to discuss how they are to be found and employed, but if anyone wishes, he may refer to Aristotle, Hermogenes, and Quintilian, who have written in great detail on these matters. We shall treat those matters that pertain to copia, but briefly, lest we seem to be writing a book, not a commentary. Accordingly, in

[67]

achieving copia, *exempla* hold first place, whether you advise, or exhort, or praise, or attack, in short, whether you desire to produce belief, to move, or to entertain. Thus, as one should obtain the greatest and most varied number of these possible and have them always at hand it will be necessary to treat them in detail. The diversity of the *exempla* sometimes depends on their source. There are past deeds and past sayings for example; and common customs of peoples are adduced in *exempla*. *Exempla* are also drawn from the differences in authors, for example: From historians, from poets, and among the latter, from the comedians, tragic poets, epigrammatic, heroic, and bucolic poets; from the writers of philosophy, of whom there are several groups; from the theologians; from sacred volumes. From the diversity of nations: In this class are *exempla* of the Romans and their institutions; of the Greeks, and among the Greeks, of the Spartans, of the Cretans, of the Athenians; likewise of the Africans, Hebrews, Spaniards, Gauls, English, German. Again from the difference of times: For some things are ancient, some of moderate antiquity, some recent, and some even current. In addition, from the quality of things: For some are military, some civil, and some acts are kindly, some brave, some wise, and so on, for this indeed is endless. Finally, from the condition of persons: Some things are of princes, some of judges, some of parents, some of slaves, some of paupers, some of rich men, some of women, some of maidens, some of boys. Thus a great number and variety of these should be gathered for each one of the places, gathered not only from from every type of Greek and Latin author, but even from the annals of the barbarians, and in fact from the common talk of the crowd. For we are moved most strongly by *exempla* that deal with illustrious events of our own past or the present day, of our own race and people, or even with inferior subjects such as women, children, slaves, and barbarians.

How *Exempla* Are To Be Treated

Furthermore, *exempla* are not only varied, but are also enlarged and amplified in handling. We shall point out several ways of doing this. First, they are enlarged by commendation. This for the most part depends on praise either of the thing or the author or the race whence the *exemplum* is derived. For example, if one should use a Spartan deed or saying, he could say by way of preface that this race had far excelled others in wisdom, and military and civil discipline, and was rich in the most noble *exempla*. If anyone cites an *exemplum* from Plutarch, he may preface it by saying that this author is one of the most authoritative of all, who, indeed, united the highest knowledge of philosophy with the persuasive skill of historians, so that in him one must see not only the credibility of history but in truth the authority and judgment of the most august and learned philosopher. Likewise, if anyone should wish to adduce the *exemplum* of M. Atilius Regulus returning to the enemy, he could introduce it in this manner: Among so many noble examples of Roman virtue, no deed was ever more fine or more praiseworthy than that of M. Atilius. It is permissible to add small laudations of this sort, either longer or shorter as the passage demands. However, only those should be added that are especially appropriate to what is in question. For example, if confidence in the *exemplum* is desired, the author will be commended for his authority and credibility. If you wish what you are introducing to appear pious, the commendation should be based on piety; and so on.

Second Method of Expanding *Exempla*

Exempla can likewise be expanded by developing them more fully or in more detail with exaggerations and amplifications. For those who desire conciseness, it will be enough to have indicated the *exemplum* in a word, as if it were well known. Cicero does this in the *For Milo*: "For neither could the great Servilius Ahala nor Publius Nasica, nor Lucius Opimius nor the Senate in my consulship be considered other than detestable if the slaying of criminals is detestable."[21]

But who aspires to copia will narrate more fully what was done, as Cicero did in the same oration: "When a military tribune, a relative of the commander, indecently assaulted a soldier in the army of Gaius Marius, he was slain by the one to whom he offered violence." And he added an *epiphonema:* For the virtuous youth preferred to act dangerously rather than to submit shamefully, and that great hero set him free, absolved of crime."[22] And in those speeches which are designed for display, it is permitted to pause longer in amplifying *exempla*, especially if the matter is of such a nature than any pleasing charm holds the hearer. For example, if one should want to make the point that travels, the viewing of many things, are conducive to the acquisition of wisdom he could, spending some time in praise of Solon, narrate in great detail how he left his state, and why, and what seas he traversed, and what strange peoples, at what risk of life, he visited, what men he met, and what marvelous things he saw, and how much time he was away and how much more famous and at the same time wiser he returned to his native land. Of almost the same kind are the *exempla* about the travels of Pythagoras and Apollo in St. Jerome, in the preface which he places before his complete text of Sacred Scripture.

[21] Cicero *For Milo* 3. 8 (Quintilian v. 11. 16).   [22] Cicero *For Milo* 4. 9 (Quintilian v. 11. 15).

CONCERNING THE FABULOUS *Exemplum*

And this same method of expanding and contracting has a place also in fabulous *exempla*. For they can be related both fully and briefly, if circumstances and propriety allow. But in the case of those that are wholly lacking in credibility, it is well to have a preface, unless we are joking, to the effect that they were composed with good reason by the wisest men of olden time, and that not without reason have they been honored by the general agreement of men for so many ages. Then we will explain what they meant: For example, if one wished to urge that that should not be sought after which is not consistent with one's nature, he would say that the ancient and wise writers perceived this with discernment and expressed it in a most fitting composition, the traditional fable of the Giants whose rash undertakings ended unhappily. Or, if one should propose that the avaricious man does not so much have what he has, as that which he does not have, he would use the fable of Tantalus with a preface. If one should propose that the reward of a wise man is that he may control the passions of the soul by reason and judgment, he would cite the passage in the first book of Homer's *Iliad* about Achilles moving his hand toward the hilt of his sword and Pallas restraining him. Likewise, if one should propose that the true glory of virtue is not achieved unless one has been tossed about by adversity and tried in various perils, he would cite the Homeric Ulysses with a preface of the kind we have discussed. Moreover, although the method of allegory is not encountered everywhere to the same extent, nevertheless, it is beyond question that in the skillful authors of antiquity, in all the creations of the ancient poets, allegory is found, either historical, as in Hercules' battle with the two-mouthed Achelous; or theological, as in the example of Proteus turning himself into all kinds of shapes, or Pallas born from the brain of Jove; or scientific, as in the fable of Phaethon; or moral, as in the case of those men whom Circe turned into brute animals by a magic potion and her wand; and sometimes one type of allegory is mixed with another. In some cases it is not at all difficult to apprehend the sense of an allegory. Who does not understand (for it is more agreeable to take examples from those that pertain to character) that the story of Icarus' fall into the sea warns one not to go higher than is his destiny? Thus doubtless the fable of Phaethon teaches that one should not undertake the execution of a task beyond his powers. Likewise, the tale of Salmoneus thrown headlong into Tartarus teaches that we should not strive after what is far above our position. The story of the flaying of Marsyas teaches that we should not contend with those more powerful than we. What else, moreover, does the story of Danae deceived by gold mean except what Horace explains: Nothing is so well fortified as to be safe from assault by money, nothing so incorruptible that it may not be corrupted by bribes? What, the labors of Hercules, except that by sweat and helping others immortal fame is gained? What, the wish of Midas, except that the avaricious and insatiable are choked by their very wealth itself? What Bacchus burning from a stroke of lightning, thrown into the fountains of the Nymphs, except that the flame of wine must be quenched by a sober element? And that is even asserted in a Greek epigram. What does the fable of Circe turning men into beasts by sorcery signify, except that those people who are not guided by reason, which is the special characteristic of men, but have given themselves up wholly to foul desires, have nothing of man except the name, but have degenerated to the nature of beasts, for instance, by licentiousness to bears, by sloth and idleness to swine, by ferocity to lions, and so on? But not to be too tedious, Eustathius, the Homeric commentator will supply any number of interpretations of this kind. Also we at one time in our youth treated these matters in a book that we wrote, *Against the Barbarians*.

Furthermore, those in this class which the poets have devised are less forced; for example, those they compose about the gods in imitation of human life, as, when Homer has Mars entrapped in chains by Vulcan, or when wily Jupiter in a dream inspired hope of capturing Troy, although he was deliberating something far different. For this is the practice of kings, to carefully spread certain rumors abroad, having purposed in their own minds something much different. And even still less forced than these, are the ones recounted in such a manner by the poets that they can be classified as history not as fables. An example of this type is Orestes, the parricide, and Pylades' friendship with him. For there are those who maintain that the thing did happen. Another example is Alcestis, by her own death warding off her husband's, which even Valerius Maximus mentions. Likewise, the death of Codrus and that of Menoeceus are included, and the death of Quintius Curtius and of the Decii. And among pairs of friends, Theseus and Pirithous, Castor and Pollux are cited. In the same class likewise belongs the story of Arion carried back to his fatherland by a dolphin, for St. Augustine affirms the story's authenticity. Certainly in Vergil and especially in Lucan, there is no doubt that many of the stories are historical. And yet many of Herodotus' are untrustworthy. And Xenophon wrote the *Cyropaedia* more as an example of education than as a trustworthy account of history. And if these are accepted as true, they are effective because they are believed, but if as fictions, since they have been handed down by the wisest and most approved authors, they are effective by the very fact that they have been devised by those whose authority has the force of precept. On the other hand,

[71]

there are in the poets *exempla* of certain and historical trustworthiness concerning Scipio, Hannibal, Augustus, Pompey, and Julius. There are, again, others which no one denies are fiction; but since it is established that they were devised for this very purpose and by great authors, they certainly have the force of *exempla*. Of this sort are the goddesses, Envy, Rumor, Mischief, and Prayers concerning whom mention was made above. In addition there are the characters that are introduced in plays, or mixed poems, especially comedies, with which the dialogues have much in common. For if one is urging that parents should beware if they sin, not to sin with children as witnesses, will not Clitipho inveighing against his father have the force of *an exemplum* when he speaks thus: "Hang it, when he has had a little to drink, what pranks of his own he tells me about. Now he says, 'Take from others the lesson that may be of advantage to yourself.' Wily man. He has no inkling to what deaf ears he tells his story."[23] Or if anyone should urge according to the answer of the wise man that one should marry a wife of the same status (as himself), otherwise if a pauper married a wealthy woman, he would marry not a wife but a master, would not Chremes in the *Phormio* be a good example, fearing Nausistrata as he would a master. Likewise, if anyone should urge that friendship between a pauper and a wealthy man is neither firm enough nor safe, would it not be effective to cite the words of Euclio in Plautus' *Aulularia,* a pauper deprecating relationship by marriage with the wealthy Megadorus: "There comes to mind, etc."[24] For the passage is very well known. Again, when you are asserting that parents act wrongly when they rage against delinquent children, although they themselves, old men, sin more seriously, would it not be well to cite the example of the just mentioned Nausistrata speaking thus: "Does it seem so shameful to you that your son, a young man, has a mistress when you have two wives? Are you not ashamed to reproach him thus? Answer me."[25] But surely it is silly for me to be citing this or that example, when all comedy is nothing but a mirror of human life. Likewise, I could quote from tragedies, eclogues, dialogues, and like forms. But I think in these notes I have indicated the way fully enough to the able. Indeed, I think *exempla* may properly be drawn not only from those places which we have mentioned, but in truth from dumb animals and even from inanimate objects. Although they seem rather to pertain to ὁμοίωσις, i.e., *similitudo*. For example, if one should exhort others to work by describing and discussing the industry of ants. Or if one should stimulate men to observe laws and civil discipline by describing the polity of the bees. Or if censuring the man averse to friendship, who

[23] Terence *The Self-Tormentor* 2. 220 seq.

[24] Plautus *Aulularia* 2. 226 *seq.*

[25] Terence *Phormio* 2. 379 *seq.*

neither loves anyone, nor is loved by anyone, you would cite the example of Delphinus, the boy of adamant; or of an eagle, burning with love for a virgin; or of a magnet attracting iron to itself. But of these things more perhaps, when we treat parables.

THIRD METHOD OF ENRICHING EXEMPLA

Besides the already mentioned ways, *exempla* of both types, i.e., the fabulous, as well as the historical, may be expanded by parable also, what is called ὁμοίωσις (and Cicero translates as *collatio*), and by *comparatio*, or *contentio*. It is a parable when a suitable *similitudo* shows that an *exemplum* which is introduced is either a simile or *dissimile*, or *contrarium*. Simile, as: Just as Camillus, having driven out the barbarians by his prowess, restored the Roman state which had been oppressed by the Gauls and brought to the extreme of ruin, so Laurentius recalled Latin letters as though from the infernal regions to their pristine splendor when they had been corrupted, buried, extinguished by the ignorance of men almost barbarians. *Dissimile*, as: A not equal debt of gratitude is owing to Laurentius and Camillus because the latter, prompted by patriotism, at the risk of his own life liberated his country from barbarians; the former, moved by desire for fame, or rather, by eagerness to censure as many as possible, did not restore an oppressed Latin language, but brought it back to fixed laws, as it were, which he learned with much pleasure by reading eloquent authors. Marcellus restored their works of art to the Syracusans when they were our enemies; Verres stole them away when they were our allies. For restoring is the opposite of stealing, and enemies of allies. Likewise, Brutus slew his sons for plotting treachery; Manlius punished the bravery of his son by death. And in Vergil: "And he, from whom you falsely claim your birth, even Achilles, did not act thus toward his enemy Priam."[26] Further, *comparatio* points out that something which has been introduced is either equal or less or greater. Less, as: "If cities have been overturned because of a profaned marriage, what is fitting treatment for an adulterer?"[27] Likewise: "Our ancestors often waged wars on behalf of merchants or shipmasters, who had been unjustly treated; what ought to be your feelings, then, when so many thousands of Roman citizens have been slain by one command and at a single moment? Because their envoys were addressed somewhat insolently, your forefathers decided to wipe out Corinth, the light of all Greece; will you suffer to go unpunished this king who imprisoned, scourged, racked with every kind of torture and put to death a consular legate of the Roman People?"[28] Equal, as in the same

[26] Vergil *Aeneid* ii. 540 (Quintilian v. 11. 14).

[27] Quintilian v. 11. 9.

[28] Cicero *For the Manilian Law* 5. 11.

[73]

Cicero: "For I myself happened to be a candidate with two patricians, the one a most unscrupulous person, the other a most virtuous and noble man. But yet I surpassed Catiline in worth; Galba, in popularity."[29] Greater, as in the *For Milo:* "They say that it is wrong for him who confesses that he has slain a man to look upon the light of day. In what city, pray, are men such fools as to maintain this? Why, in that one which saw as its first case on a capital charge the trial of Marcus Horatius, the bravest of men, who, although the city had not yet been freed, was acquitted by the Roman people in assembly in spite of the fact that he confessed that he had slain his sister by his own hand."[30] Accordingly, in that which is properly called *exemplum* (there is, however, *commemoratio* of a deed done, or just as if done, useful in persuasion) there is either very brief exposition (an example is St. Jerome's: *Memento Daretis et Entelli*) or broader application through *collatio*, simile, *dissimile, contrarium*, or through pointing out what is equal, greater, or less. Now this *collatio* is drawn from all circumstances of things and persons. Artifice of style is useful; with words and figures suitable to the occasion, some details are purposely made light of, others are emphasized. Furthermore, whoever wishes to draw out an *exemplum* most fully will develop individual parts of a *similitudo* or *dissimilitudo* and compare them with one another as Cicero does in the *exemplum* we repeated above concerning the murdered envoy. For he places after it a *collatio* of the parts: "They would not tolerate encroachment on the liberty of Roman citizens; will you disregard their death? They avenged the verbal violation of the law of embassy; will you leave unnoticed the death by every torture of your ambassador? Watch out lest, as it was their greatest honor to leave to us so glorious an Empire, so it be your greatest shame to be unable to protect and preserve what you have received."[31] And it is proper to do this as fully as you please, if you compare many circumstances with each other. For example, if one should urge some one to bear the death of his son with restraint, and from the *exempla* of the pagans should hold up as an example some woman who bravely bore the death of several children, after narrating the story, he would make his comparison thus: What a weak woman was able to bear, can not you, a bearded man, endure? She with her sex overcame a mother's emotion; will you be overcome by a different affection? She bore the loss of several children with unbroken spirit; will you lament inconsolably the death of one? Consider also the fact that all her sons perished simultaneously by shipwreck, surely a death without glory; yours fell bravely fighting

[29] Cicero *For Murena* 8. 17 (Quintilian v. 11. 11).
[30] Cicero *For Milo* 3. 7 (Quintilian v.

[29] 11. 12).
[31] Cicero *For the Manilian Law* 5. 11-12.

in battle. She had nothing to which she might honorably ascribe the fate of her sons; you gave your son to your country. They in truth perished utterly; your son will live forever in immortal glory. She gave thanks to nature that she had once been the mother of so many sons; you remember only that you have lost your best son. She had no hope of replacing her loss, a task greater certainly than her womb could then accomplish; you have a fertile wife and vigor still unimpaired and hearty. Therefore, where a barbarian woman excelled, will not you, a Roman man, excel? Will what she, unskilled in letters, was able to scorn, break you, so gifted in letters, so great a professor of philosophy. Finally, that fortitude of spirit which a pagan woman showed, will not you a Christian man exhibit? Although she believed that nothing survived the funeral pyre, nevertheless she considered grief unbecoming; do you who have learned that only they truly live who have worthily departed this life cry out ceaselessly that your son has perished? And what she surrendered to nature with a calm spirit, do you not surrender to God when he takes it back? She submitted bravely; do you resist God? From this model it is sufficiently clear, I think, how *exempla* should be compared, although in actual cases, since there is a greater abundance of circumstances, it is easier to find various *contentiones*. The suggestion should be made, incidentally, that *sententiae* and *epiphonemata* can be mingled in this type of *contentio* with a pleasing effect. For example, in this same *exemplum* after the first *collatio*: Can not a bearded man endure what a weak woman was able to? *sententiae* could have been added: Nature made a distinction in sex, do you not make a distinction in spirit? No one expects superior fortitude from a woman. Unless a man is strong in spirit he is not deemed worthy the name of man. Man signifies both a more robust sex and a strong spirit. It is a disgrace for one who wears a beard to be surpassed by a woman in stoutness of heart. Likewise, after that *contentio*—she had nothing to which she might ascribe the fate of her son with honor; you gave your son to your country—*sententiae* something like this could have been added: It is a great solace for grief to have something to which one can honorably ascribe fate. A son is given to nothing more rightly or more gloriously than to one's country. Again after the *contentio*—they truly perished utterly; yours will live forever in immortal glory—something like this could have been added: A life of honorable fame is far happier than one of common breath. The life of the body is both miserable and generally, even though no accident happens, short, and also something shared with beasts; the brilliant and eternal life of man carries him back to the strengthening comfort of God. In the same way *sententiae* could have been added to the separate parts of the *collatio*. But it is sufficient to have pointed these

[75]

out in passing, for we will speak concerning *sententiae* in their proper place.

Concerning Parables

Now indeed, even if those who like to split hairs make this distinction between the parable and the *exemplum,* that the *exemplum* pertains to the deeds of particular men, while the parable is a *similitudo* derived from the things that are done by nature or chance or in some way related to them, for example, Atilius Regulus returning to the enemy is an *exemplum* that the obligations of religion and promises should be fulfilled, but a ship methodically raising or lowering its sail, shifting it from one side to the other according to the winds, is a parable teaching that the wise man should conform to circumstance and accommodate himself to current conditions—nevertheless, the method of amplification by parable is the same as we have explained for the *exemplum.* For sometimes, it is briefly indicated as: You don't see that your sails ought to be trimmed; or, stop drenching the side; so that it may be either an allegory or a metaphor. At other times, it is developed more fully and adapted more clearly, as Cicero does in the *For Murena:* "But if those who have just come into port from the deep are wont with great zeal to advise those just leaving port on the weather, pirates, and geography, because it is natural for us to befriend those who are entering upon the same perils that we have undergone, how ought I to feel, seeing land at last nearby after a great storm, toward him whom I see must undergo the greatest storms?"[32] Again in the same speech: "As they say among the Greek musicians, those who are not able to sing to the cithern, sing to the flute, so we see those who are not able to rise to the status of orators, sink to the study of law."[33] St. Jerome imitated the above parable of Cicero in a certain letter to Heliodorus in this way: "And I, not having ship and cargo intact and not as one ignorant of the waves and inexperienced as a sailor, utter this warning, but as one lately cast up on the shore by shipwreck, with faltering voice announce to those about to sail: On that sea the Charybdis of luxury devours salvation; there with virginal countenance the Scylla of passion, smiling, lures chastity to shipwreck. Here is a barbarian shore, here the pirate Devil with his comrades carries chains of bondage. Do not trust him; do not be careless, even if the sea smiles like the quiet waters of a lake, even if the topmost surface of the quiescent element barely curls, this plain holds great mountains; within is peril; within is the enemy. Quick with the halyards, lower the sails. Let the cross of the ship's yard be fastened

[32] Cicero *For Murena* 2. 4 (Quintilian v. 11. 23).

[33] Cicero *For Murena* 13. 29 (Quintilian viii. 3. 79).

on the bows; that calm is a storm."[34] Here if anyone wishes to compare the separate perils that threaten morality through vices, or wrong-doing, or in other ways with the details that ordinarily make for crises in the life of sailors, and to point these out through comparison as greater or lesser, and through *dissimile* or *contrarium,* and finally to embellish them with suitable *sententiae* and *epiphonemata,* he will indeed copiously amplify his speech, as in this example: As the more precious a thing is, the more diligently is it wont to be guarded and the more carefully expended, so the greatest care must be taken of time, than which nothing is more precious, lest any of it pass without some profit. For truly, if guardians are customarily given to those who recklessly squander jewels and gold, what insanity will it be, then, to waste time, the most beautiful gift of immortal God, either in idleness or shamefully in dishonorable pursuits? For what do you lose when you lose time, if not life? What can be dearer than life? And when a single small gem has disappeared, you call it a loss; when a whole day has vanished, that is, a good part of it, do you not call that a loss? Especially since, when jewels are lost they can be obtained again else-where but the loss of time is irreparable. Moreover, when the former are lost to you, generally they are a gain to someone else; but the loss of time is not converted to the profit of anyone. There is no loss from which someone does not realize some gain, except the loss of time. Furthermore, there is the fact that loss of the former kind of wealth has often been a salvation. For riches generally provide the resources of vice, so that it is better to have squandered them rashly than to have preserved them carefully. The more honorable is the use of a thing, the more disgraceful is its waste. But there is nothing finer, nothing more splendid, than good hours well spent. Although you guard the former as carefully as possible, nevertheless, often either accident snatches them away or man carries them off, so that the loss renders you unfortunate to this extent, but not base as well. But loss of time, since it does not happen except by your own fault, renders us not only unfortunate but infamous, indeed, guilty of the worst type of infamy as the blame for it can be assigned to no one but the one who suffers the evil. With the former you could have bought property or buildings, but not a good mind. With the latter, in addition to the other orna-ments of the soul, you will be able to gain immortality. There is no part of life so brief that in it some great step toward happiness could not be made. Finally, for wrongly expending the former you would perhaps have to render an account to your father, but for hours wrongly spent, to God.

[34] St. Jerome *Letters* 14. 6.

But this is sufficient indication of how greatly it is possible to expand *collatio* if anyone wishes to compare separate circumstances in this way and embellish them. For *dissimile* there is the same method of treatment, of which the following is an example: For although a new ship is more useful than an old, it is not so with friendship.[35] And as she is to be praised who distributes money freely to many people, it is not so with her who gives her beauty. For although in a relay race he who takes the torch is swifter than he who hands it over, in war the general who receives the army is not better than the one who turns it over to him.[36] Further, the way in which *collationes* may be drawn from every sort of thing has been pointed out above.

CONCERNING *Imago*

Εἰκών, which the Latins call *imago*, seems closely related to *collatio*, and if you amplify it, a *collatio* is the result. For example, if you should say: As an ass is not driven away from his fodder with a club unless he is glutted, so a warrior will not rest from killing until he has sated his spirit, that is *collatio*. But if you said someone threw himself upon the enemy like a dragon or a lion, that is εἰκών; or that Achilles came into battle with his arms blazing like fire or like the sun, that is *imago* rather than *similitudo*. As Homer is most prolific in both, so is he most successful. Yet εἰκών makes more for vivid presentation, or emphasis, or enjoyment of the speech, than for proof. But although the use of *exempla* and similes contributes to those same things, nevertheless these figures are unusually helpful in producing conviction, especially when they are employed through induction, which the Greeks call ἐπαγωγή. In this type the Platonic Socrates is very rich. An *exemplum* is employed inductively in this way: Tell me, what profit did his brilliant eloquence finally bring to Demosthenes? As everyone knows, besides other misfortunes, a most unhappy and miserable death. Again, what reward did it bring to Tiberius and Caius Gracchus? To be sure, death, wretched and dishonorable. What, further, to that so highly praised Antony? In truth he was stabbed most cruelly by a bandit's dagger. What reward did it bring to Cicero, the father of eloquence? Was it not breath, bitter and wretched? Go now and strive through many sleepless hours of work to attain the highest glory in eloquence, which for outstanding men has ever been destruction. Simile is employed inductively in this way: Will not a sailor discuss navigation better than a doctor? or will not a doctor expound the science of healing more accurately than a painter? or will not a painter speak better than a shoemaker concerning the science of colors and shadows and lines? Will not a charioteer talk better than a sailor about how

[35] Quintilian v. 11. 26.   [36] *Rhetoric for Herennius* iv. 46. 59.

to drive a chariot? And if a great many such examples are brought together, they make it seem entirely probable that everyone will speak
better on that subject which he knows better. Then an appropriate
similitudo is added: But what of the orator who claims that he will
speak best on any subject? The *exemplum* about Aspasia and Aeschines
is well known.[37]

Concerning the Demonstrative *Contentio*

There is also a kind of general *contentio*, especially in the demonstrative type, when for the sake of praise or censure we contrast one
person with another; for example, in order to praise Julius, the Roman
pontiff, one might contrast him with Caius Julius Caesar and compare
the good deeds of the former with those of the latter. Or on the other
hand, to censure, one could compare evil deeds with evil deeds. Likewise, to praise Maximilian one could contrast him with Marcus An-
tonius Imperator. There is also *comparatio* of things. For example,
someone praising history could compare its services with the good
deeds of those who enlarged the state by war; or, desiring to praise
poetry, might set side by side and consider its advantages and those
of philosophy. There is also the *comparatio* of one to many. For example, if one should desire to magnify the praises of history, he would
compare history with all the most esteemed studies. And here there
is a double method: For either you make light of the good things
about one and magnify those of the other; or you exaggerate the praises
of the one, but in such a way, nevertheless, that at the same time you
represent as preferable, or at least equally desirable, what you have
undertaken to praise. In censuring you emphasize the faults, but in
such a way that you show what you are attacking to be even worse,
or equally bad. In these you must be careful that whatever is employed for the *comparatio* be acknowledged and notable. For example,
you would compare a good prince with Trajan, or Antoninus, the
Philosopher, but a bad one with Nero or Caligula; a slanderer with
Zoilus or Hyperbolus, a detractor with Dipsas or Regulus; a man effeminate in his pleasure with Sardanapalus. Moreover, the copia of
the *comparatio* will be increased if, as I have just mentioned, several
persons or things are employed for the praise or censure of one person
or thing. For example, to praise a prince, you would take from many
princes the thing in which each especially excelled: From Julius Caesar,
good fortune and presence of mind; from Alexander, magnanimity;
from Augustus, affability; from Titus Senior, civility; from Trajan,
moral integrity and humanity; from Antoninus, contempt of glory; and
so on. A similar procedure is followed in censuring. Also, in denouncing

[37] Quintilian v. 11. 27-9.

bad temper, you would compare it with extreme drunkenness, with delirium, or with epileptic or demoniac disease; in cindemning wantonness of speech, you would compare it with the condition of a man afflicted with a pestilence, with a serpent's breath which contains a most powerful poison, or with the exhalation of certain pools or pits, which causes sudden death. *Judicia,* which the Greeks call κρίσεις, are also, as we have said, classified as *exempla.* And they are the *sententiae* of famous writers, of peoples, of wise men or renowned citizens. A great number of *judicia* can be collected from the celebrated poets of antiquity, and also from historians, from philosophers, and from private letters. For these again exhibit the same variety that was pointed out in *exempla.* Certain of the Greeks, among them Stobaeus, have worked collecting these *judicia* from all sources. Likewise, the apothegms of wise men are useful, of which type are the sayings of famous men repeated by Plutarch. This type is varied. For if it is a question of subject, there are the military and the philosophical; if a question of persons, there are kings, wise men, and the common people; if a question of quality, there are serious sayings, facetious sayings, and pointed sayings. To this class also belong proverbs, either those taken from authors, or popular sayings. For I do not see that public practices of peoples differ from *exempla* in any respect. Certainly, oracles and responses of the gods are included in *judicia,* just as if you should assert Socrates was a wise man, because he was so judged by the oracle of Apollo.

CONCERNING *Sententiae*

There is a class of *sententiae,* not that, indeed, devised by writers, but by us for the purpose of the present work. They may be scattered through all parts of a speech; and even one place often contains several *sententiae.* For they may occur both in narration and in appeals to the emotions, not only in proofs, but often as a device for making transitions. And if they are employed appropriately, they contribute a no small copia to a speech, and that not without weight or charm. There are, moreover, various forms of *sententiae.* Some are universal in application, as: Envy is its own punishment. Others are not suitable unless related to a subject, as: Nothing is so popular as kindness.[38] There are others which refer to a person, as: The prince who wishes to know all things must ignore many.[39] Another type is simple, as: Love conquers all things. Another has a reason added or combined, as: In

[38] Cicero *For the Manilian Law* 1. 31. 51.

[39] Quintilian (quoting D. Afer) viii. 5. 3. Erasmus loses the point of the saying by changing Quintilian's *ignoscere* (ignore) to *cognoscere* (learn). In translating I have restored *ignoscere.*

every contest the more resourceful, even if he receive injury, nevertheless, because he is more powerful, seems to inflict it.[40] Some are double, with opposing parts, but with no added reason, as: Complaisance makes friends; truth, hatred.[41] Some are of different parts, as: Death is not miserable; the approach to death is.[42] In this type if a reason be added to each part, the *sententia* becomes quadripartite, in this way: Those who think they ought to overlook the sins of the young, are mistaken. This is the first part of the *sententia;* to this a reason is appended: Because their age is an impediment to good inclinations. Then a third part will be: But those take the wise view who severely chastise youth. And again a reason is added, as: in order that they will want to acquire at the earliest age those virtues by which they can preserve all life. Although this exemplum is in the *Rhetoric for Herennius,* nevertheless, I do not find it at all pleasing.[43] However, it is not difficult to compose another of this sort: Industry becomes youth. The reason is added: for it would be shameful to waste in idleness and in disgraceful pleasures the gifts which nature allotted to those years for acquiring useful arts. But prosperity becomes old age. To this also a reason is added: so that by it the age more destitute of nature's defences may in some measure be supported by the props of external things. Likewise another: Destitute old age is miserable; ignorant old age is disgraceful. For it is miserable to be in need at that time when natural weakness especially requires the support of money, and disgraceful to be ignorant of the best things at that time when it is not fitting to learn but rather to teach. Again a *sententia* may be stated directly, as: A miser lacks what he has as much as what he does not have.[44] There is a figurative *sententia,* as: I have been able to preserve, do you ask whether I can destroy?[45] In its simple form it was: It is easier to destroy than to preserve. There is a common *sententia* of things: As it is easy to do harm, it is more difficult to do good. There is one adapted to persons. In this case the *sententia* is of such a nature that it may be less immediately apparent, as is that one of Cicero: "Your fortune, Caesar, has nothing greater than the power, nor your nature anything better than the wish to preserve."[46] There is also an implied and partly concealed type of *sententia,* as in Vergil: "And she is consumed by a hidden fire."[47] For Ovid explained: "A covered fire burns hotter."[48]

---

[40] Sallus *Jurgurtha* 10 (Quintilian viii. 5. 4.)

[41] Terence *Andria* I. 1. 41 (Quintilian viii. 5. 4).

[42] Quintilian viii. 5. 5.

[43] *Rhetoric for Herennius* iv. 17. 25.

[44] Publius Syrus *Sententiae* 486 (Quintilian viii. 5. 6).

[45] Quintilian viii. 5. 6.

[46] Cicero *For Ligarius* 58 (Quintilian viii. 5. 7).

[47] Vergil *Aeneid* iv. 2.

[48] Ovid *Metamorphoses* i. 502 (Quintilian viii. 3. 47).

Likewise, this is used in narration: The majority party overcame the better.[49] You can expand this by saying: it generally happens that the majority party overcomes the better. There is another type of *sententia* which the Greeks call ἐπιφώνημα; Quintilian, *acclamatio*. This is a climax in the form of an exclamation at the end of a narration or proof. An example of the former is found in Vergil: "Such a great labor it was to found the Roman race";[50] of the latter, in Cicero: "Does the speech, then, of those very men whose freedom from punishment is your title to clemency spur you on to cruelty?"[51] And yet not every *epiphonema* is necessarily a *sententia*, although it generally is, but anything that, subtly added at the close of a period, strikes the ear, can be called an *epiphonema*. And this type is characteristic of epigrams, as in the epigram about the sheep giving suck to the wolf cub: Nature is never confused in her functions. Whence in Martial a poem often ends with an *epiphonema*, as: "Either stay awake or dream about yourself, Nasidienus."[52] Likewise: "Do you want me to tell what you are? You are a great busybody."[53] Also, Valerius Maximus makes frequent use of this type, and Seneca commonly concludes his letters with an *epiphonema*. And there have been those who considered the use of *epiphonema* so exceedingly agreeable that they thought it necessary to end every passage, every idea, with an *acclamatio*. But the use of *acclamatio*, as of all *sententiae*, ought properly to be restricted to those instances where the subject demands them, or definitely allows them. There is also the *noema*, a type of *sententia*, which is understood rather than expressed. An example of this type is the answer to the brother who brought action for retaliation because his sister had cut off his thumb while he slept, although she had often bought him off from the gladiatorial school: You deserved to have a whole hand. For, "so that you might fight again in the school" is understood.[54] A similar one is that of Hortensius, if I am not mistaken, who said that he had never been restored to the good graces of his mother and sister. For it is understood that he had never had a quarrel with his mother or sister. There are recently devised types of *sententiae*: those that depend on the unexpected, the allusive type, those transferred from another context, those that are produced by doubling, and those from opposites.[55] If anyone should want them he may find examples of these in Quintilian.[56]

---

[49] Livy xxi. 4.
[50] Vergil *Aeneid* 1. 3 (Quintilian viii. 5. 11).
[51] Cicero *For Ligarius* 10 (Quintilian viii. 5. 10).
[52] Martial *Epigrams* vii. 54.
[53] Martial *Epigrams* ii. 7.
[54] Quintilian viii. 5. 12.
[55] As may be seen by a study of the material cited in the preceding notes, Erasmus follows Quintilian very closely in this whole discussion of

CONCERNING *Expolitio*

Expolitio seems to be related to that type of *sententia* which we have shown above consists of four parts. For this is the name given to the device whereby we dwell a long time on the same point, varying the same *sententia* in different ways, and at the same time enriching it. We may do this by changing of words, by expressing the same thing many times in different words and figures; by change in delivery, when it is expressed with different facial expression, gesture, and voice; by changes in point of view, when we have someone else say something we have just said in our own person, but have them say it a little differently; or when we express more vehemently and passionately something that has been argued rather calmly. But the most copious *expolitio* consists of seven parts: general statement, reason, double *sententia*, to which a reason also double can be added, *contrarium*, simile, *exemplum*, conclusion. For example: A wise man will shun no peril in the service of his country.[57] Because it often happens that he who has been unwilling to die for his country necessarily perishes with it. And since every advantage has been accepted from his country, no disadvantage ought to be considered grievous in its service. This is the first part, in which the whole matter is set forth simply and is supported by reasons. To this is added a double *sententia*, augmented by as many or more reasons. Therefore, they who flee the peril that they ought to undergo in the service of their country act foolishly. This is the *sententia*, to which is subjoined the reason. For they are unable to escape it and are discovered to be ungrateful to the state. Then a contrasting part of the *sententia* is added. But those who at their own peril fend off the perils of their fatherland are to be deemed wise. Next, reasons are added: since they render to the Republic the honor they owe it, and prefer to die in defense of many rather than with many. Now the *contrarium* is added to this: For it is extremely unjust when you have preserved with the help of your country the life you received from nature, to render that life to nature when she requires it and not to give it to your country when she requests it, and when you are able with the greatest virtue and honor to die for your country, to prefer to live through dishonor and cowardice, and although you

sententiae. This particular sentence comes nearly verbatim (except that Erasmus does not include Quintilian's examples) from Quintilian viii. 5. 15. The phrase *nova sententiarum genera*, which I have translated into English as "recently devised types of *sententiae*," is Quintilian's. In transcribing from his notes on Quin-

tilian, Erasmus evidently failed to remark the incongruity of using *nova* with reference to types of *sententiae* that were already more than a millenium old.

[56] Quintilian viii. 5. 15-9.

[57] This example of *expolitio* is taken from the *Rhetoric for Herennius* iv. 42. 54, and more fully iv. 44. 57.

are willing to expose yourself to peril in defense of friends, parents and other relatives, to be unwilling to go into danger in defense of your country in which both they and that most sacred name of fatherland are included. Then a simile is used: And just as he ought to be despised who in sailing puts his own safety above that of his ship, so he ought to be censured who in his country's danger consults his own rather than the common safety. A *collatio* of a *similitudo a majore* is added. Many people have been saved from shipwreck; no one is able to swim away safely from the shipwreck of his country. To this is joined *exemplum:* And Decius, who is said to have sacrificed himself in behalf of the legions by throwing himself into the midst of the enemy, seems to me to have understood this. To this are added *sententiae:* Because he gave up his life he did not perish. For he bought the noblest thing with the commonest; he gave his life, and received his country. Losing his life, he gained glory that, prolonged by age with the highest praise, becomes brighter every day. Then finally is added the conclusion, like an epilogue: Now if it has been both demonstrated by reason and confirmed by *exemplum* that one ought to undergo danger in defense of his country, those ought to be considered wise who shun no peril in defense of their country's safety. Accordingly, it is fitting that boys who are being instructed to acquire copia be trained with themes of this sort. However, I do not especially approve even this example from the *Rhetoric for Herennius,* except that it does indicate the method. But it can be treated with even greater copia if you accumulate more *sententiae,* reasons, similes, and *exempla.*

CONCERNING APOLOGUES

Apologues come very near to the class of the fabulous, except that they give greater pleasure and persuade more effectively. They give pleasure by a certain witty imitation of customs; they convince because they place the truth before your eyes as it were. Country people, the uneducated, and anyone else whose ways have a flavor of the golden age are especially captivated by them. The apologues under the name of Aesop are especially celebrated, and he has been considered one of the wise men for this very reason, although Quintilian thinks that they were written by Hesiod, and they were certainly the work of someone of unusual talent.[58] Wherefore it is not to be wondered at that Menenius Agrippa recalled the Roman plebians from a most dangerous sedition by devising for that purpose an apologue about the members of the human body conspiring against the stomach, as Livy relates.[59] And Themistocles persuaded the Athenians not to elect new magistrates, with the fable about the fox covered with flies. Almost

---

[58] Quintilian v. 11. 19.   [59] Livy ii. 32 (Quintilian v. 11. 19).

[84]

anyone can compose this kind of tale for a given purpose, but to compose aptly not only must you have considerable talent, but also you must have studied thoroughly the natures of living things (for they are of infinite variety). Moreover, as far as the use of apologues is concerned, they can be indicated in a word, just as *exempla* may, especially if the apologue is well known. For example, you may say: If uneducated people censure and condemn your writings, do not be troubled; they will certainly be approved by the most learned. For is it to be wondered at if the Aesopian cock scorns a precious stone? Or you may say: No enemy however impotent and humble should be disregarded or disdained; the Aesopian eagle did not scorn the beetle with impunity. Or this: Rely on your own good deeds, not on the glory of your ancestors, lest there happen to you what befell the little crow of Aesop. They may be amplified, moreover, by a prefatory commendation. At times we commend the author himself, at other times apologues in general. For example, Aulus Gellius in treating the fable of the crested lark: "Aesop, that Phrygian author of fables, etc."—(the passage is readily accessible).[60] They may also be amplified by lingering over a description of the natures and forms of the animals and things which you introduce, since, indeed, this type of description is received with pleasure and is also pertinent to liberal education. For example, you might describe the shape of a beetle, then how it is born from dung, and the way it pushes dung forward, with its hind legs erect, and other things of this nature. In the same way you might describe how the eagle holds sway over the race of birds, is the armor bearer of Jove, is not hurt by lightning, does not blink at the brightest rays of the sun, is borne beyond the clouds in swiftest flight, and whatever tends to exaggerate the lowliness of the beetle, or extoll the nobility of the eagle. This theme, in fact, we have treated for sport in proverbs. Moreover, in this matter if anything has been attributed to any animal in the stories of the poets it must not be disregarded; for example, that wolves are sprung from Lycaon and partridges from a youth, that the swan is sacred to Apollo and sings most sweetly at the hour of its death, that the raven was the messenger of the same god and was made black from white because of its laziness. Nor must the stories related in the histories about unusual actions of animals be overlooked; as for example, the one about the eagle who fell in love with a virgin, in Pliny, or the one about Bucephalus, the horse of Alexander the Great, and so on, for we are simply indicating a method. Then when we come to the apologue itself we may narrate the story somewhat fully and extensively. This will be done without tedium if by a

---

[60] Aulus Gellius *Attic Nights* ii. 29.

kind of humorous imitation we adapt something characteristic of the life of men to the usages of the fable, and if besides we devise *sermones*, *sententia* and sayings according to the same method. There is a most apt example in Horace's *Satires:* "A country mouse is said to have received a city mouse in his poor hole, old host, old friend, rough and careful of his store, yet he loosed his frugal soul in hospitality, etc." (The passage is readily accessible.)[61] There is also an example of an expanded apologue in Apuleius about the fox and the crow; and one in Aulus Gellius about the crested lark. On the other hand, it does not matter at all whether you place what is called ἐπιμύθιον, i.e., interpretation of a fable, at the beginning or at the end. It is permissible to begin with this and to end with it, provided only that variety of speech results.

CONCERNING DREAMS

Some people use dreams also, which perhaps should not be used except for display, for example, the dream of Lucian; sometimes we describe them as real visions for the sake of exhorting or deterring. Such is the composition of Prodicus about Hercules hesitating which way of life to undertake, an arduous one of virtue or an easy one of pleasure; and the similar one about Momus who found it reprehensible in man that the maker of the world had fashioned a curved heart in him, and had not added a window, in the ox, that he had not added eyes on the tops of its horns, so that it might see what it struck. The famous dream of St. Jerome about being scourged with a lash because he was a Ciceronian seems to be of this type. In our youth we also indulged in this kind of composition as a pastime.

CONCERNING FICTITIOUS NARRATIVES

Now fictitious narratives of events, if they are presented as true for the sake of persuasion, ought to be composed with the highest possible degree of plausibility. And there are well-known examples of the rhetorician's art which have an air of probability, for example, the fable about Memmius in Cicero, and perhaps the one about Vulteius in Horace. I think that some writers have taken too much pleasure in this type, and, relying on the credulity of the people, have introduced into Christian literature as most true some extremely foolish miraculous wonders. Furthermore, as regards those that are devised for the sake of humor, the farther they are from the truth, the more they delight the spirit, provided only that they do not resemble the absurdities of old women, and can by erudite allusions capture the attention of the learned. To this class belongs the *True Histories* of Lucian; and Apu-

[61] Horace *Satires* ii. 6. 79-83.

[86]

leius' story of an ass is an example of it, and *Icaromenippus* and most of Lucian's extant works, and also almost all the arguments of the ancient comedy, which please not by imitation of reality, but by allusions and allegories. For there is no doubt that that type of fiction that presents a shadowy image of reality is related to the parable. An example of this is the story of Plato about the cave in which certain people are chained and take pleasure in shadows as though they were actual things.

CONCERNING THEOLOGICAL ALLEGORIES
But whenever we exhort to piety, or dissuade people, *exempla* from the Old and the New Testament, i.e., the Gospels, will be very helpful. These can be treated variously by use of allegory and they can be adapted to the customs of men, to the body of the Church, bound to and in harmony with Christ its head, to the heavenly communion, also to the early ages of the nascent faith, and to these our own. But we will treat these matters more fully and in greater detail in a little book that we have undertaken concerning theological allegories. Almost all of these are classified as *exempla*, on which we have dwelled at rather great length because from this ornament especially the material of copia is derived But before we leave them it seems best to make still a few more brief suggestions.

METHOD OF COLLECTING *Exempla*
How any *exemplum* can be variously adapted by means of *similitudo, contrarium, comparatio*, hyperbole, epithet, *imago*, metaphor or allegory has been shown above. Now we shall point out the method by which we can have the greatest number of them on hand and in ready money, as it were, a plan, to be sure, not so noble as profitable; and if we had only followed it in the old days as a boy (for it occurred to us then too) I see how much of moment it would have added to our literary studies. But nevertheless, it is the part of honest genius not to begrudge youth advantages either because fortune denied them to you, or you did not gain them by diligence. Therefore, whoever has resolved to read through every type of writer (for he who wishes to be considered learned must do that thoroughly once in his life) will first collect as many topics as possible. He will take them partly from classes of vices and virtues, partly from those things that are especially important in human affairs, and that are accustomed to come up most often in persuasion; and it will be best to arrange these according to the principle of affinity and opposition. For those that are related to one another automatically suggest what should follow, and the same thing is true of opposites. Suppose, for example, the first general classification is Piety and Impiety. Under the former heading will be placed

[87]

the several particular kinds. First, there is piety toward God; second, toward the fatherland; third, toward parents or children, or even toward those whom we ought to honor in place of parents—as teachers and those by whose kindness we have been taken care of. The opposite of these is Impiety. Superstition is related to these and might be added here. And here a very wide field is opened up having to do with strange cults of the gods and various ceremonies of different peoples. Likewise, improper indulgence of children by parents, which is false piety.

The next title might be, if it seems suitable, Fidelity; you may divide this into its particular kinds: fidelity to God, human fidelity, fidelity to friends, servant's fidelity to their master, fidelity to enemies. There are the same number of headings for Infidelity.

Next might be the title *Beneficence*. When you have added under this its particular kinds, there remains *Gratitude*. That is not, to be sure, a subdivision of the former, nor again its opposite, but is very closely related to and like a consequence of it. All of these topics can be treated along the following lines: First, what piety is, how it differs from other virtues, what is peculiar to it, in what ways it is preserved or violated, by what things it is strengthened or corrupted, what it profits man. Here a field of *exempla* and *judicia* is opened up. But anyone may make an orderly list of the virtues and vices for himself, following his own judgment, or if he prefers, he may seek it from Cicero or Valerius Maximus or from Aristotle or from St. Thomas. Finally, if he prefers, he may follow an alphabetical order. For that is not of great importance, although I would not want him to put into his lists all the particulars of this kind, so minutely specified, but only those which seem to be required frequently in speaking. This indeed he may learn from the divisions of cases, namely demonstrative, hortatory, and forensic. In general the headings in Valerius Maximus and some in Pliny are in this class; for the rest, those general classifications selected apart from the vices and virtues are partly *exempla* and partly commonplaces. The former class are generally of this sort: Extraordinary longevity, vigorous old age, senile youth, unusual happiness, remarkable memory, sudden changes in fortune, sudden death, voluntary death, unnatural death, extraordinary eloquence, unusual riches, famous men of humble birth, subtlety of intellect, extraordinary physical strength, extraordinary appearance, distinguished character in a deformed body, and innumerable others of this sort. And under each of these it will be necessary to place those things that are opposites and those that are related. For example, the opposite of extraordinary eloquence is extraordinary inability to speak. Related topics are euphony, skill in gesturing, dramatic ability, and anything else of this sort. The latter class, on the other hand, are of this sort: It makes a very great difference to what studies you become accustomed as a boy. With whom you live is of great importance. Offending anyone in the matter of his appearance is easy, reconciliation is difficult. It is safest to trust no one. Love as though on the point of hating; you will hate as though on the point of love. He gives twice who gives quickly. His own conduct determines the fortune of every man. The slow wrath of kings; the perilous friendship of princes; war attractive to the inexperienced; the unsafe fellowship of royalty; and the best viaticum of old age, learning. But why continue to enumerate when there are thousands of them? Accordingly, the student should select those which seem especially suited for speaking. To this group belong also those that depend on comparisons, whether celibacy is happier than marriage, a private life than a public one; whether a monarchy or a democracy is preferable, the life of the learned or of the uneducated. Then if any of the above seem to be related to a virtue or a vice they may be placed under the appropriate heading. For example: He gives twice who gives quickly; nothing is dearer than what is bought with prayers; he has been benefited by giving who has given to a deserving person; nothing is so lost as what is given to an ungrateful person; reproaches destroy the kindness of a good deed; and such as these can be entered under the heading of Liberality. But, lest a disorderly mass of materials produce confusion, it will be useful to divide more general classifications into several subdivisions. The classification Liberality, as we are using it, for example, may be so divided if you add under it: service promptly and quickly rendered; appropriate kindness; kindness conferred on the deserving and undeserving; reproachful kindness; mutual kindness; and any others judged suitable. For we are suggesting these simply for the sake of illustration. Then after you have collected as many headings as will be sufficient and arranged them in the order you wish, and have placed the appropriate divisions under each, and to the divisions have added the commonplaces or *sententiae*, then whatever you come across anywhere in any author, especially if it is very noteworthy, you will immediately mark down in its proper place whether it be a fable, an apologue, an *exemplum*, a strange occurrence, a *sententia*, a witty or otherwise unusual expression, an adage, a metaphor or a parable. This method will also have the effect of imprinting what you read more deeply on your mind, as well as accustoming you to utilizing the riches of your reading. For there are those who hold a great many things in their minds, as though stored up in the earth, although in speaking and writing they are wonderfully destitute and bare. Finally, whenever the occasion demands, the stuff of speech will be ready to hand, as if safe nests had been built, whence you can take what you wish. Furthermore, no learning is so far removed from rhetoric that you may not enrich your classifications from it. For from mathematics, which seems to be most remote, *similitudines* are taken. For example, a wise man, happy in his wealth, not dependent on anyone else, constant and unmoved in his own virtue whatever way the winds of fortune blow, is compared with a sphere everywhere similar to itself and with a tetragon resting on four corners equally whithersoever it falls, to say nothing of the fact that theologians frequently take from mathematics an interpretation of mysteries, because of a certain concealed resemblance between things and numbers. From physics not only parables, but also certain *exempla* are taken. A parable would be this: As the lightning most often strikes the highest mountains, so the greatest power is liable to the worst calamities. Likewise, as lightning melts bronze, leaving wax untouched, so the spirit of princes ought to rage against the rebellious and the mutinous, but be clement toward others. Elephants, through modesty copulating in secret, would be an *exemplum* to use in a discussion of modesty in married people and concealment of passion. And dolphins accompanying their mature offspring for a long time and not allowing their young to go out unless someone older, either a pedagogue or a guardian, is present, would be an *exemplum* to use if one should be advising with what great care parents ought to protect and direct that first and critical age of young people. And so the student, like the industrious bee, will fly about through all the authors' gardens and light on every small flower of rhetoric, everywhere collecting some honey that he may carry off to his own hive. Since there is such a great abundance of subjects in these, a complete gleaning is not possible, and he will be sure to select the most important and adapt them to the pattern of his work. There are some which can be adapted not only for different, but even for opposite uses, and therefore should be noted down in several places. For example, if you should be treating the incurable cupidity of a miser, you would rightly adapt the fable of Charybdis. Likewise, if you were discussing insatiable gluttony, or the inexhaustible lust of a woman, the same fable would certainly be appropriate. Likewise, the apologue of Aesop about the goat and the fox going down into the pit together will be appropriate to illustrate either foresight, by which it results that you would not undertake an affair unless you have first considered within yourself by what method you can settle it, or to the kind of false friends who although they appear to be consulting the interests of a friend, are nevertheless chiefly concerned with their own interest. Moreover, the death of Socrates provides not only an *exemplum* that death should not be feared by the good man, since Socrates drank the hemlock with such a cheerful countenance, but also

[90]

that virtue is liable to injury from envy and is not safe when surrounded by evil men. It also provides an *exemplum* that the study of philosophy is useless or even pernicious unless one conforms to the general mores. And here this fact may itself be developed both to praise Socrates and to censure him. For he should be praised who, condemned through no crime of his own but solely through envy, was so bravely indifferent to death; he should be censured who by his useless study of philosophy and neglect of the general mores brought the bitterest grief upon his friends, wife, and children, and calamity and destruction upon himself at an age when others are accustomed to be of service to their country, a protection and at the same time a source of pride to their relatives, and therefore to be truly wise, having abandoned finally the stern doctrines of wisdom to adapt themselves to the studies and opinions of the multitude and to serve the time, as the saying goes. Now if you examine the parts of the *exemplum* how many commonplaces may be drawn from it? He was accused through the envy of Anytus and Melitus, two of the most corrupt citizens. The commonplace is: Truth creates hatred. There is another: Outstanding virtue wins envy. And another: With judges, regard for aristocracy for the most part carries much greater weight than respect for virtues. Yet another: Nothing is more shameless than wealth if it is coupled with vicious character. For what more absurd than for those men, disgraced by every crime, to call Socrates to justice? Likewise there is another commonplace: Not anything at all is fitting to anyone whatever. Therefore, Socrates did not cast himself at the feet of the judges. And indeed, it was not right that he who had throughout his life taught that death was not to be feared unless it was shameful should now as if in fear of death be an abject suppliant. And for the same reason he did not avoid the trial or in the middle of it choose exile, nor finally, when there was an opportunity, was he willing to escape from prison, lest he seem himself to act at variance with his own principles. And from that part where, when about to die he argues so calmly and so undisturbedly, when he drinks the hemlock with the same expression he was accustomed to drink wine, when on the point of death he jokes with Phaedo, reminding him to sacrifice a cock to Aesculapius, may be drawn the commonplaces: Death is even desirable to those who are conscious of having lived a virtuous life. From the same part may be drawn the commonplace: The sort of life a man has lived is most clearly apparent at death. Likewise, there is an *exemplum* of a man steadfast and unalterable. For the countenance and speech which were Socrates' throughout his life were his when on the point of death. There is a third part. While Socrates is in prison, Alcibiades is never there for a visit, nor Agathon, nor Phaedrus; but Crito is, and Phaedo and

[91]

Simias. And this is the commonplace drawn from it: In times of danger it finally becomes clear who are true friends. For petty men consult their own interests when confronted with common duties. A fourth part is: He argues at length with his friends about the immortality of the soul; when he has spoken to his wife and children briefly he dismisses them. The commonplace is: A philosopher ought to be touched by the ordinary affections lightly—this harmonizes extraordinarily well with Christ's teaching. A fifth part is: Immediately after the death of Socrates the popular fury was turned upon his accusers; a golden statue was erected to *Socrates Beloved*. The commonplace will be: The crowd hates and loves thoughtlessly. Another: We hate virtue when it is present, but when it is taken away from our sight, we seek for it enviously. Likewise another: False glory perishes with life, the splendor of virtue becomes brightest after death. Here I think it is clear to how many uses this same *exemplum* can be adapted. A parable may be handled similarly; for instance, how many similes could be taken from sailing? As a storm makes clear who is the best pilot, so calamity makes clear who is the best leader. Likewise: As no one entrusts the helm to the most friendly, but rather to the most competent sailor, so no one will consign the direction of the Republic to him who desires it most, but rather to him whom he judges most fit. Likewise: Just as sailors take in sail when the winds are too strong, and when they are light, spread their folds more widely, so when affairs prosper exceedingly, the spirit should be tempered lest it become haughty; but when fortune is unfriendly, the spirit should then expand and be sustained by fortitude and hope of future good fortune. Likewise: Whenever it is not possible to hold a straight course through a storm, then we ought to strive by tacking back and forth to reach that place whither we wish to come. Likewise: Whenever the violence of a storm is too great for the sailors' skill, they take in the sails and throw out the anchor; in the same way it is sometimes necessary to yield to the raging multitude, until through the power of oratory it begins to be manageable. Similarly: Just as the sailor does not always keep the sail in the same position, but now raises it on high, now takes it in, now turns it to this side, now to that, in whatever way the winds demand, so the wise man ought not to pursue the same course in life everywhere, always, and under all circumstances, but ought to adapt his countenance, his speech, and his habits to existing circumstances. Likewise: Just as in great storms the most skilled sailors sometimes permit themselves to be advised by even the unskilled, because in such emergencies some things come to the mind one way, some another, in the same way a good king in the Republic's great perils will not refuse to hear the advice of anyone. Likewise: As in the slightest danger the helm is handled by that pilot who has experienced the greatest perils, so the safest condition for a state is under that prince who has been trained in the gravest emergencies. Likewise: As he who controls the rudder does not think that he adequately performs his duty unless he looks about him and warns anyone what should be done, so he does not act like a prince who does not direct and be responsible for the duties of the lower magistrates also. Likewise: Just as a sailor would be insane if through hatred of some whom he carried on a ship he allowed the ship to be lost, since in the wreck he could not be safe himself, so he would not be of sound mind who because of partisanship did not defend the safety of his country, without the safety of which he could not himself be safe. Likewise: As sailors are accustomed to throw out the sacred anchor only in the most savage storms, so only in the gravest perils and well-nigh desperate circumstances should recourse be had to extreme remedies. But surely it is foolish for me to treat of these further, since you now see that several thousand *similitudines* can be derived from them. Sometimes too the same part of a *collatio* is developed for different purposes, for example, if you should compare the frequent changes of the moon to the vicissitudes of fortune, or to the instability of human life, or to the inconstancy of fools. Indeed the same *sententia* also is turned to various uses, as: An eloquent companion is as good as a vehicle on a journey. Life is more pleasant if you do not live alone, but have the companionship of a charming and agreeable friend. Again: You should always carry around some good book, by the reading of which you may dispel tedium. Likewise: if a spirit cheerful and conscious of no evil accompanies you, no part of your life will know tedium. He is the best traveling companion who speaks of cheerful things. But if he recalls to you the memory of shameful deeds, he bores you to death. The procedure for proverbs and apothegms, the uses of which we have shown in the beginning of a collection of proverbs, is the same. In the same way, some of them should be written down simultaneously in different places, or at least noted there. For it will be sufficient to have once indicated in a few words, the place in the authors where they can be found, especially if they cannot be set forth briefly. But now, so that by this example the matter may be made more clear, let the heading be Inconstancy, or inconsistency of character, and let us try how many subjects can be collected under this heading. First, from the stories of the poets, I will take Mercury, accustomed to assuming various shapes, as he is the crafty god, sometimes living among the inhabitants of the upper world, sometimes among those of the lower, sometimes among mortals, also performing various duties, now acting the part of Ganymede in offering the cup to Jove, now carrying messages, now leading souls down to

[93]

Charon, now rendering service to tradesmen and advocates, sometimes holding the cithern, and sometimes wearing his two-colored striped cap, finally, delighting in many names. In Aristophanes' *Pluto* he is called crafty, tradesman, wily, presider over the roads, president of the games; in Homer and Hesiod, the one who leads the souls down, Argus-Slayer. Also he is called Cyllenian, and exceedingly useful. I will take Vertumnus, a god who is named because he is continually changing his shape. I will take Proteus, changing himself into every sort of strange thing. From Aristophanes' *Frogs* I will take Empusa, i.e., a kind of lesser divinity continually appearing under a different form. Likewise I will take Morpheus, accustomed to assume whatever appearance he wishes, and Circe with her magic potions and magic wand, turning men into shapes of various animals. For the wicked are not of unvaried character, but are driven by various desires. I will take Opportunity, a changeable god never resembling himself, and like to this one, the Rhamnusian goddess. I will take Jove, now an eagle, now a swan, now a bull, now turned into a golden shower; and also the Chimaera, with the head of a lion, the body of a maiden, the tail of a dragon; and that varied monster which Horace fashions in the very beginning of his *Art of Poetry*. And I will bring in two-faced Janus, and triformed Geryon, and Bacchus, to whom the poets attribute fickleness and levity of character; and such a one Aristophanes pictures him in the *Frogs*. And whatever others there are that convey the effect of strange variety. I will bring in Ulysses, who assumes any character at will according to circumstances. And for this reason Homer at the very beginning of his work calls him versatile in character. Then from natural philosophy I will take a *similitudo* of the moon, never returning to us with the same face, now half-full, now full, now waning, now waxing, now yellowish, now ruddy, now white, now coming ahead of the sun, now following it. I will take a *similitudo* of the vernal or autumnal sky, now cloudy, now clear, now calm, now disturbed by winds. I will take a *collatio* of the sea flowing down from the tidelands and returning again in constant alternation, especially the Euripus, flowing back and forth with wondrous speed seven times a day and night. I will add the Polypus, whose changeableness is proverbial. I will add the chameleon repeatedly changing its color, and the panther, with its variegated, many colored spots, or any other animal of this sort, and the slippery eel. I will add the nature of childhood which changes hourly. I will add further the peculiar inconstancy of women, and the multitude, moved by a slight disturbance, also the wondrous mobility of quick silver, a reed, bending lightly to every breath of air, the lightness of dry leaves and of a bit of feather, the pliability and soft nature of wax, the changeableness of dreams, the rapid, whirling motion of a

[94]

wheel. I will bring in the vane that it is the custom to place on the topmost point of towers and temples where it indicates the wind by turning. I will add the scales with easy movement inclining on this side and that. I will add vermiculated mosaic work, exhibiting wondrous variety of small varicolored squares. Some are even fashioned from natural qualities; for example, one might compare the spirit of a changeable man, now thinking about this, now about that, to a polished mirror hung in the busiest forum, which shows a varying picture of countless figures, a crowd hastening hither and thither; or to glass which, whatever color you bring near it, seems to copy it; or to hanging steel, which when magnets are brought near on both sides, one of which attracts the steel to it, the other repels it, is dragged this way and that in quick movement nor ever is at rest; or to a sphere spinning on a flat surface. Then from history in turn I will take the native changeableness of the Greeks, which Juvenal describes, the perfidiousness of the Allobroges, the Carthaginians, of a like inconstancy of character, the Scythians, changing their pastures from day to day and never dwelling in a fixed abode, the staff of Moses repeatedly turned into different forms, Aristippus playing any character whatever, as (according to Horace) "every color became him, now wearing the mantle of the cynics, now the royal purple";[62] and also half-white, that one whom Lucian mentions. I will take Catiline of varied nature, from Sallust; Hannibal, from Livy; from Valerius Maximus, those whose lives followed different courses in youth and in old age. From the third *Satire* of Horace I will take Tigellius:

> There was nothing consistent in him.
> Often he ran as though fleeing from the enemy.
> Very often he walked as if he were bearing offerings to Juno.[63]

From the comedies will be drawn an example of feminine inconstancy, Sostrata in the *Brothers:* "Ah me are you in your right mind? Do you think that this should be revealed anywhere?" and a little later: "Never in the world, I won't, I'll disclose it."[64] Phaedra, returning suddenly from the country, will represent the inconstancy of lovers; Antiphus from the *Phormio,* childish inconstancy. But it is of no use to pursue this. From the tragedies I will borrow Phaedra, with her varying moods, now willing, now unwilling; likewise Medea, before the slaying of her sons, tormented by various emotions; Byblis and Narcissus from Ovid; from Vergil, Dido, when Aeneas is already preparing his departure. And scattered through the works of the poets there are innumerable characters of this type. From the fables I will choose that countryman

[62] Horace *Epistles* i. 17. 23.
[63] Horace *Satires* i. 3. 9.
[64] Terence *Adelphae* 336-37, 343 *seq.*

who, to the Satyr's wonderment, from the same mouth used to breathe now hot, now cold; and any other there may be. For here we are only indicating the method. From proverbs I will borrow Diana, wandering over all lands; likewise, field of wind; more versatile than the buskin (the tragic actor); more varied than the hydra; Libyan beast, and others similar. For we have ourselves collected places in the proverbs whence such things can be sought: a rock which is frequently turned is not covered with moss; a tree which is often transplanted does not grow. Again, from apophthegms I will add what was said against Cicero: To sit on two chairs. And what was written against the same man by Sallust: "He says one thing while standing, another while sitting." From Homer, I will take the changeable, who adapts himself to everything. For thus he terms Mars, who is wont to change parties, and who sides now with these, now with those. From Ovid, if I am not mistaken, comes this: "And she is only constant in her fickleness."[65] From Horace, "lighter than cork"; and, "he changes square to round"; and, "changeable as the wind, at Rome I love Tybur, at Tybur, Rome."[66] From Plautus: "Lighter than a water-spinner."[67] From Terence's *Phormio:* "I will, I won't, I won't, I will, what is said is not said," etc.[68] From Euripides: "For your thoughts are changeable: now these, formerly those, presently others."[69] Now it is apparent, I think, how much material of this type can be collected from so many writers. This method with *sententiae* is the same, and you may not only take these from authors, but also make up new ones yourself; and if you add to all of these a like number of their opposites, having added under each those closely related, you see how truly great a storehouse of speech it will be. But so varied is its use, which we shall demonstrate with more care in a work on letter writing, that there is nothing which you cannot in some way adapt to the enrichment of speech. The *contraria* may be used also either in irony, *dissimile,* or *comparatio*: in irony, as if someone should call Socrates, who throughout his life always appeared with the same countenance, a man never resembling himself. In *dissimile,* as if you should say Julius Caesar never regretted any deed. He never decreed anything which he did not straightway repeal. In *comparatio,* if you should say, as the great Cato whom Cicero called stubborn could not be diverted from an opinion, so this man cannot abide by one opinion. Furthermore, those that are closely related, are with slight modification adapted to allied subjects. For example, that passage of

---

[65] Ovid *Tristia* v. 8. 18. Erasmus has slightly modified the text of Ovid which reads: *Fortune* is constant only in her fickleness.

[6] Horace *Odes* iii. 9. 22; *Epistles* i. 1.

100, and i. 8. 12.

[67] Plautus *The Persian* 2. 2. 62.

[68] Terence *Phormio* 5. 950 *seq.*

[69] Euripides *Iphiginia et Aulis* 332.

Persius: "Dwell with yourself."[70] For although properly it fits him who undertakes things greater than are his destiny; nevertheless, because discontent with one's destiny is related to inconstancy, it can be turned this way, especially since Seneca writes: "I consider the ability to be firm and live with oneself the most telling proof of a balanced mind."[71] These same ones indeed can also be turned to praise. To praise a man well disposed at all times, versatile, and competent, you can take from your collection on the topic of inconstancy the polypus that changes its color according to the appearance of the ground under it. You can take the Euripus and say that this sea is not so versatile as the talent of this man; you can take flame, unable to remain still; you can take the sky, continually of different aspect; you can take the reed, bending whenever the breezes blow. You may say that it is the part of a wise man to change his ideas and way of life in accordance with circumstances that arise, in accordance with time and place, and that senseless rock and brute earth alone are unchangeable, but that among living creatures, the more outstanding anything is the more mobile it is. In all nature the more distinguished anything is, the farther it is from rest. The basest element is earth which does not move; but water is mobile; air more mobile; fire, yet more mobile than this; the sky most mobile of all. Hence the mind of man from ancient times has been called air and fire. On the other hand, fools, sluggards, and dullards are called stones and lead, to which the designation of constancy is especially suited. Through commonplaces of this sort you may draw many things from the material of constancy for censuring, and from that of inconstancy you may adapt many to praise. But about these we shall speak again at a more opportune occasion, since there has been but brief mention of them here. Now we shall take up the remaining methods of amplifying speech.

On the Multiplication of the Parts of a Speech

An oration may be enlarged by increasing the number of its parts. For as he who wishes to be most brief uses as few parts as possible, so he who desires to amplify will take care to add those legitimate parts prescribed by art. For although in general the purposes of an orator are three, to instruct, to please, and to persuade, anyone who likes brevity, content with one, will only instruct, which is done by narration and adducing proof; and he who likes copia will employ everything at once, and that in all parts of the speech, not only in the peroration or exordium. Likewise, he who desires brevity can be content with the narration, or, even omitting this if the pattern of the

70 Persius *Satires* 4. 52 (Lactantius ii.   71 Seneca *Moral Epistles* ii. 1.
    2. 18).

case allows, with the proof alone. And this also, although it cannot be wholly omitted, yet can be abridged and limited. On the other hand, he who aims at copia not only will use those six, exordium, narration, division, proof, refutation, peroration, but also as concerns the exordium, will develop its places rather fully at the beginning of the speech and then throughout the oration, wherever the subject permits, will intermingle certain small exordia, by which he may render his audience well disposed, attentive, and receptive, or dispel tedium, or soften beforehand something he is about to say. This type, moreover, occurs very frequently. We keep our audience in a receptive mood most effectively by suitable transitions, several formulae for which we have suggested in the above commentary. An example would be: You have heard that he gained public office by bribery, corruption, bloodshed, defilement, and the foulest arts. Now I will show that what he disgracefully acquired, he has administered more disgracefully. Attention is generally renewed by these methods: These things are important, but they are trifling compared with those that I am now about to say; and, now I am coming to the very heart of the matter. Accordingly, I ask that you hear these things with the utmost possible attention. And, but perhaps I have delayed overlong on these matters; the rest I will explain briefly and clearly, if you will grant me your hearing and attention as you have done up to now. And, I will repeat in somewhat greater detail, but I am going to use such words that you will hear me with profit and pleasure. And this may be done in other ways also; for hundreds of them can be composed according to the nature of the subject. Tedium is dispelled or prevented in this way: I ask that you listen attentively. Perhaps at first appearance what I am treating seems insignificant, but if you will give me your attention for a short time, you will see that the greatest dangers to the Republic are without doubt hidden under this seeming. And, I ask your forbearance for a short time; soon I will make clear whither these things lead. And, now you will hear something unheard before this. And, you will hear something, of all things especially amusing. Good will is renewed by those same methods by which it is gained. Moreover, at times we introduce argument in the exordium, if there is anything to be refuted which would otherwise be prejudicial to one making the rest of the speech, but this is not done except by a plan based on the circumstances of the matter.

The narration can be effectively enriched by a figure which some call *sermocinatio*, by which we put into the mouth of one or several persons a fitting speech, as Homer portrays aged Priam dissuading Hector from battle, and later portrays Hecuba and Andromache, Hector's wife, discouraging him from battle, and Hector answering them, with the individual traits of each character wonderfully preserved. Nor is anything more admirable in the writers of histories. For it is permitted to historians by universal consent to put speeches into the mouths of people. I speak of the pagan historians; whether the same may be permitted to Christians is doubtful, except that a similar practice is seen in the history of the seven Maccabees and is followed by others who have written the lives of the martyrs. St. Ambrose in his life of St. Agnes seems to have permitted himself the same license. The narration is filled with every kind of argument and appeal to the emotions, except that it is more fully developed elsewhere, and also is enlarged by ἐπιδιήγησις, that is, as Quintilian shows, a repetition of the narration, relating a second time more fully and with more profusion of ornament a subject that has already been set forth briefly and simply.[72] This is done either to excite indignation or pity. Furthermore, the narration is also expanded by adding a digression. And Quintilian permits this if the excursus is so closely related that it is a sort of conclusion to the narration; for example, if the end of a narration has been bitter, he may develop it further as though in a spontaneous burst of indignation, and this even in serious cases and those involving risks.[73] On the other hand, in a subject prepared for display, once the subject has been set forth, nothing forbids digression in any case where it is especially plausible and pleasing; by it you may at the same time banish the tedium of the narration, and by the charm of your words render your hearers more eager for the coming proof. What sort of places these may be has been pointed out above.

The proposition may be expanded in the first place if instead of the simple proposition we use the double or multiple, even if one is sufficient, because one thing gives rise to another; for example, if he had done this he was deserving of reward rather than punishment. Or, this thing is neither honest nor expedient nor can it be done without the greatest peril; but if it should be wholly honest, expedient, and safe, yet it cannot be done, as we shall show in detail. We may also expand the proposition if our statement is not entirely bare but is made interesting by arguments thrown in here and there and by appeals to the emotions. There is an example of this in Cicero's *For Milo*: "I have related these things, judges, exactly as they happened. A conspirator was vanquished. Violence was overcome by violence, or rather audacity was crushed by courage." Then he interposes an appeal to emotion: "I say nothing of what you, what all decent men gained; let that count not at all in favor of Milo, who was fated when born not to save even himself without saving the Republic and you." Then he piles up argu-

[72] Quintilian iv. 2. 128.   [73] Quintilian iv. 3. 4 *seq.*

[99]

ments: "If this could not be justified, then I have nothing to say in his defense. But if reason commands this to learned men, and necessity to barbarians, and custom to the human race, and nature itself to wild beasts, that always by whatever means they are able they should ward off all violence from their persons, their heads, and their lives—you cannot judge this to have been a criminal act without at the same time judging that all who have attacked robbers ought to perish either by the weapons of the latter or by your votes." Straightway he returns to emotional appeal: "If he had thought so, certainly it would have been more desirable for Milo to have bared to Claudius his throat which the latter had attacked not once only, nor then for the first time, than to be slain by you for not having given himself up to be slain by Claudius."[74] And likewise, in what follows in defining the controversy, (the passage is a famous one), he repeats the whole of the arguments that he had used in the exordium. Although this was more permissible for Cicero because he had treated several questions in the exordium, nevertheless, the same thing may be done elsewhere by the apt interposition of words, especially in the enumeration or exposition, which is another part of the division about which we have said something above when we were treating the proposition. For example, if in urging Cicero not to accept his life from Antony at the price of burning his *Philippics*, you should speak thus: First consider, my Cicero, whether for such a little time, since a long time cannot be left to such an old man, it is worthy of you by burning your most glorious title to fame to heedlessly destroy the immortal fame of your genius which you produced with such great labor as a crowning ornament to all your works. Then consider whether a brave man, who ever prized liberty above all things, should endure that he owe his life, the best of all things and that in which all things are, to that monster to whom no free man would wish to be obligated under any pretext whatever. Finally, he should see it is not the part of a wise man in such a matter to trust a most treacherous enemy who has never kept faith with his friends, and not to foresee what is apparent to even a blind man, that the most crafty scoundrel, Antony, is doing nothing except to utterly destroy Cicero. For it could be set forth simply in this way: First, life is not of such value; then, it is a wretched thing to owe one's life to an enemy; finally, Antony wants to ensnare not to save. But if a proposition seems rather harsh, one ought to soften this beforehand by a small exordium, as it were; for example, if you proposed to praise the teaching of Plato concerning the community of wives you would say that you do not avoid what you know offers a most absurd subject in the opinion of everyone. You will

[74] Cicero *For Milo* 11. 30 (Quintilian
iv. 4. 2).

request that they defer their judgment until they have heard all of the arguments, that you do not doubt but that when the matter is fully set forth they will come to a different opinion. Let them only consider that, whatever this is, it was the considered opinion of a great philosopher, and one who in other things earned the name of divine because of the excellence of his genius. But what is true regarding the appearance of men is also true in the judgment of things; if you look at certain ones casually from afar, nothing is more charming—dross, plainly deceiving the eyes. But if you observe them more closely and steadily, then that which a little before was wonderfully pleasing to the eyes begins to greatly displease them. What more ridiculous than the Sileni unless you explain them? But if you explain, what more august? So truth lies concealed in hidden places, and in judging things one ought not to follow popular report by which always the worst things are accustomed to be considered the best. Accordingly, having put aside for a little while the usual opinion and the one deeply impressed on their minds, let them weigh the subject itself carefully in judgment and not make up their minds one way or the other before they have heard all of the arguments. For there are some things which seem foolish by themselves, but if one observes their relationships with one another he will at length perceive the concord and harmony of truth. Small prefaces of this sort, suitably composed according to the nature of the subject, are sometimes useful in preparing the mind of a listener for the argument that is to follow.

Now, besides the methods of enriching we have pointed out above, proofs are amplified by undermining an opponent's argument in advance and by asseveration. We undermine an argument in two ways: First, by proposition, by which I mean not those statements that compass the whole of a subject, but, for example, the summaries of individual parts, or conclusions, which it is the habit of orators to place at the beginning of arguments and to repeat more emphatically at the end in an appeal to the emotions or as an epilogue. This type has been discussed in previous chapters. Furthermore, we can set these forth in such a way that by this figure of speech we either destroy belief or win it. An example is found in Cicero's *For Milo:* "But before I come to that part of my speech which deals specifically with the question before us, I think those accusations which have been constantly tossed about in the Senate by enemies and in public meetings by scoundrels, and just now even by the prosecutors, etc."[75] By using the term enemies and scoundrels, he has already destroyed much belief in his opponent's proposition. Then by use of irony he disparages the proposition itself:

[75] Cicero *For Milo* 3. 7.

"They say that he who confesses the slaying of a man has no right to look upon the light of day." For those harsh words, "they say that he has no right to look upon the light of day,"[76] must be uttered in mockery for "he should be punished." Secondly, preparations of this sort are joined to the separate parts of arguments: since indeed in the same place Cicero, on the point of refuting the proposition by means of *exempla*, prepares the way thus: "In what city, indeed, can you find men stupid enough to make this claim?" Then he adds the *exemplum* of M. Horatius, who, when he had slain his sister, was acquitted. Different from these are asseverations, which although they are not arguments, yet often have the weight of an argument if they are intermingled with the proofs; as, who is so blind that he does not see this? who so shameless that he denies it? And, he is too foolish to need rebuttal, for who does not understand, etc.; and, put aside all shame; and, dare to deny; since this is the case and this after all is shamelessness, etc. Individual arguments are enriched by special epilogues which recall to the hearer in a few words the whole reasoning just brought to his attention so that the conclusion follows with greater force; this is a frequent practice of Cicero's because he develops the point of his argument in considerable detail. An example of this type would be that from his oration *For the Manilian Law:* "Therefore consider whether you ought to hesitate to enter with all zeal upon this war to defend the glory of your name, the safety of your allies, your greatest tribute, and the fortunes of a great number of the citizens, together with the State."[77] Then those arguments are enlarged by amplification in digressions, so that we may add to individual proofs their own appeal to the emotions, for which a conclusion has been fittingly chosen. If we wish that to be copious, we may make this conclusion double, so that the chief arguments are at the same time recapitulated in an epilogue and every sort of appeal to the emotions is employed throughout. One may take these from Aristotle and Quintilian; and, indeed, the poets do this admirably. The more forceful ones, which the Greeks call πάθη, are abundant in Homer's *Iliad* and in the tragedies; less striking examples, which charm rather than move deeply, are found in Homer's *Odyssey* and in the comedies. Although in the *Iliad* and in the Greek tragedies πάθη is frequently employed (for thus the Greeks term comic appeals to the emotions), Latin tragedy uses this type more sparingly. *Delectatio* should be classified with appeals to emotion although this ought to be used not only in the peroration but throughout the speech whenever the subject permits. Aristotle describes at length and in detail in his classification of appeals to the emotions what is likely to

[76] Cicero *For Milo* 3. 7 (Quintilian v. 11. 12).   [77] Cicero *For the Manilian Law* 7. 19.

please an audience; and Cicero has written concerning witticism; and Quintilian on jests, treating the methods of joking. *Delectatio,* which is taken from comic appeals to emotion, has a place especially in narration, either because such appeals present matter graphically or because they are appreciated by all sorts of people. For who does not read with pleasure Homer's account of how Andromache ran to meet Hector in full armor at the city gate by which he was to go forth to battle; she was not alone (for that is not becoming to modest matrons) but handmaidens accompanied her, one of them bearing in her arms Astyanax, the son of Hector, especially dear to his father and (as Homer adds) as fair as a star, wherefore through him the wife would overcome the feelings of her husband. Hector quietly smiled at the sight of the boy; Andromache, standing nearby, reached out her right hand and called him by name. Then after appropriate words on the part of each, when Hector reached for the infant to kiss him, the latter, frightened by the gleaming armor and the crest waving at him from the top of the helmet, shrank back into his nurse's arms, crying. His father and mother laughed at this. But Hector took his helmet from his head and laid it on the ground, and then embraced and kissed the child. Soon, having blessed him, Hector handed the boy to his mother who took him to her sweet smelling bosom, smiling through her tears. This moves Hector to compassion, and, supporting his wife with his hand, he consoles her, calling her by name, and then he replaces his helmet. She returns home in obedience to her husband. There the whole house is filled with the weeping of the women, who did not believe that he would return from battle; and so though he was still alive, they mourn him as dead.[78] Epithets interspersed here and there add no small charm to this passage: *Hector of the many colored helmet;* and, *famed Hector longed for his son; well-girded nurse;* and, *crest of horse hairs;* and, *beloved father and respected mother;* and, *gleaming helmet;* and, *dear son;* and, *beloved wife;* and, as we have mentioned, *sweet smelling bosom;* and, *crest of a horse's tail.* This excellence is the chief reason why no one has his fill of reading Homer, but is led on by constant pleasure. These are the appeals to emotion concerning which Horace wrote:

> And a play with characters aptly sketched,
> Though lacking in charm and force and art,
> Delights the people more and holds them better,
> Than verses empty of thought, and sonorous trifles.[79]

There are several excellent narrations of this sort in Cicero; for example, in the *Philippics,* concerning Antony: "The tribune of the people

[78] Homer *Iliad* vi. 392 *seq.*   [79] Horace *Art of Poetry* 319 *seq.*

rode in a war chariot; the lictors, crowned with laurel, went before him; and among them a female mimic was born in an open sedan chair, etc."[80] For it is sufficient to indicate the passage. And there are others in the same oration, how with covered head he carried love letters to his mistress; how as consul he ran in the Lupercalia. And a pleasing effect is produced when not only the action but also the behavior of the actors is described. For example, in the *Against Piso:* "For they are written out so cleverly and learnedly that the clerk, who returned them to the treasury, when the records were written out in full, murmured to himself while scratching his head with his left hand: 'The count indeed, by Hercules, is clear, the money is gone.' "[81] Or that one: "You answer, one eyebrow raised to your forehead, the other lowered to your chin, that cruelty does not please you."[82] These sometimes make for belief in what is said when the details that are added as if unnecessarily have the appearance of simplicity. Quintilian admired the narration of Cicero in the *For Milo:* "Although Milo had been in the Senate on that day, when he was dismissed from the Senate, he went home, changed his shoes and clothes, and waited for a short time while his wife was making the usual preparations."[83]

There are likewise figures that are important to humor in a speech, which it is no great trouble to seek from the precepts of the art, and could not be treated by us except in many words. Allusions also give pleasure but only to those who recognize them. Also they must be used only when the occasion is suitable.

Epilogue

Accordingly, that person to whom laconic brevity in speech is pleasing, following the example of the Attics especially, will abstain from prefaces and appeals to emotion; he will set forth his subject simply and cursorily; he will not make use of every argument, but only the chief ones, and those he will employ not developed at length, but compactly, so that there will be an argument implicit almost in each separate word if anyone wants to develop it. He will be content to have instructed; he will abstain from amplifications, asseverations, similes, *exempla, sententiae, epiphonemata, fabulae,* apologues, allusions, witty sayings, unless any of these is so necessary that it cannot possibly be omitted. Likewise, he will avoid all figures that make a speech full, distinguished, pointed or ornamented, or pleasing. He will not treat the same subject in several different ways and he will set forth details in words so full of meaning that much more is understood than is heard,

[80] Cicero *Philippics* 2. 23. 58.
[81] Cicero *Against Piso* 25. 61; Plautus *Trinummus* 2. 4. 17.
[82] Cicero *Against Piso* 6. 14.
[83] Cicero *For Milo* 10. 28 (Quintilian iv. 2. 57).

and one thing can be inferred from another. On the other hand, he who pursues copia will be eager to amplify details, generally by the methods I have discussed.

WHAT SHOULD BE AVOIDED BY BOTH

But let each beware lest in striving for his goal he fall into the closely related vice, a thing that is commonly done. Let the lover of brevity see to it that he not do only this, i.e., say few things, but let him say the best possible things in the fewest words. And he who is pleased by that Homeric expression, *few indeed,* let him take pleasure in this also, which immediately follows, *very acutely.* And who approves *not verbose,* should not overlook this also, which is added immediately, *not random in speech.* For nothing so suits brevity of speech as propriety and elegance, and if simplicity be added to this, obscurity, a vice which is wont to go hand in hand with the inclination to brevity, will be avoided. But here again care should be taken lest the speech be dull, since it is enlivened with no emotional appeals. In the same way the subject should be so clearly presented that in itself it impresses on the mind some points that are not spoken aloud; in addition, it should be seasoned with every Attic charm. Special care should be taken that in our zeal for brevity we do not omit things that should be said. On the other hand, he who seeks copia ought likewise to employ discrimination in his choice of words and subjects and figures, lest his reasons be futile; his *exempla,* unsuitable; his *sententiae,* lifeless; his digressions, too long and too inappropriate; his figures, harsh and forced. Accordingly, he ought to consider his method of arrangement and disposition of utmost importance, lest his whole speech be thrown into disorder and confused by an undigested mass of materials. And everywhere tedium should be lightened by variety, cheerfulness, and humor. Variety is most effectively gained by figures and by them also, cheerfulness; humor, from those precepts which Cicero propounded. There are, moreover, special varieties of parts not to be neglected; hence, it is useful to have formulas for a great many exordia on hand. And there are many methods of narration; there are diverse forms of arguments; nor is the nature of appeals to emotion simple; but these ought to be taken from the precepts of the rhetors. Also it should be pointed out that we do not strive for the same amount of copia everywhere. For in certain places it cannot be profitably employed. But setting aside those places which by their nature do not admit of copia, we should select the especially fruitful and tractable parts, unless perchance to make a test or display of talent it is desired sometimes to make an elephant from a fly, as they say. Just as Favorinus praised fever; and Sinesius, baldness; and as we have praised folly in

[105]

an encomium, and the Aldine anchor in proverbs. Indulgence should be allowed in the classroom since youth naturally runs to excess. However, where it is not a question of practice composition, but of a serious matter where risks are involved, there, a rhetor who is not foolish, having considered the matter, will judge the proper measure of copia from its usefulness to the case.

Peroration

I had added an example of a theme in compressed form and one of the same theme more fully developed, which I do not include here, lest the addition appear too great a burden. It is now in a book dedicated to the most illustrious younger prince William, Duke of Cleves, with the title: *On the early and liberal education of youth.*

FINIS

INDEX

Chapters and Headings

Book I

That the Aspiration to Copia Is Dangerous............................. 11

By Whom Copia Was Developed and by Whom Practiced............... 12

How Authors Have Indulged in a Display of Copia..................... 13

To Whom Unrestrained Copia Has Been Attributed As a Fault............ 14

That It Is Characteristic of the Same Artist to Speak Both
Concisely and Copiously 14

Concerning Those Who Strive for Either Conciseness or Copia Foolishly.... 15

That Copia Is Twofold 15

For What Things This Training Is Useful.............................. 16

By What Methods of Training This Faculty May Be Developed.......... 17

First Precept Concerning Copia 18

The First Method of Varying by *Synonymia*......................... 19

    Low Words 20

    Unusual Words 21

    Poetic Words 21

    Archaic Words 21

    Obsolete Words 21

    Harsh Words 22

    Foreign Words 22

    Obscene Words 22

    New Words 23

The Words Peculiar to Different Ages 24

Method of Varying by *Enallage* or 'Ετέρωσις......................... 25

    Number 26

    Person 26

    Voice 26

    Case 26

    Species 26

    Form 27

Method of Varying by *Antonomasia* 27

Method of Varying by *Periphrasis* 27

    Etymologia 27

    Notatio 28

    Finitio 28

Method of Varying by Metaphor 28

    Deflexio 28

    From the Irrational to the Rational 28

    From the Animate to the Inanimate or *Vice Versa*............... 28

    From the Animate to the Animate 28

    From the Inanimate to the Inanimate 28

[107]

Reciprocal Metaphors 29
Method of Varying by Allegory 30
Method of Varying by *Catachresis* 30
Variation by Onomatopoeia 31
Method of Varying by *Metalepsis* 31
Method of Varying by Metonymy 32
Method of Varying by Synecdoche 33
Method of Varying by *Aequipollentia* 33
Method of Varying by Comparatives 34
Method of Varying by Change of Relatives 34
Method of Varying by Amplification 35
Method of Varying by Hyperbole 35
Method of Varying by Μείωσις, i.e., *Diminutio* 35
Method of Varying by *Compositio* 36
Method of Varying through Σύνταξις, i.e., *Constructio* 37
Method of Varying through Changing the Figure in Various Ways.......... 37
Practice 38

Book II

First Method of Embellishing: Enumeration of Details.................... 43
Second Method of Varying: Enumeration of Antecedents 46
Third Method: Enumeration of Causes 46
Fourth Method: Enumeration of Results 47
Fifth Method: Imaginative Description 47
    Description of a Thing 47
    Description of a Person 50
    Description of Place 54
    Description of Time 55
Egressio, Sixth Method of Amplifying: Wise Digression 55
Seventh Method: Epithets 56
Eighth Method: Enumeration of Circumstances 57
Ninth Method of Enlarging: Amplification 58
Tenth Method of Amplifying: Rhetorical Propositions 60
Eleventh Method: Accumulation of Proofs 66
    Commonplaces 67
    How *Exempla* Are To Be Treated 68
    Second Method of Expanding *Exempla* 69
    Concerning the Fabulous *Exemplum* 70
    Third Method of Enriching *Exempla* 73
    Concerning Parables 76
    Concerning *Imago* 78
    Concerning Demonstrative *Contentio* 79
    Concerning *Sententiae* 80

Concerning *Expolitio* 83
Concerning Apologues 84
Concerning Dreams 86
Concerning Fictitious Narratives 86
Concerning Theological Allegories 87
Method of Collecting *Exempla* 87
Twelfth Method: Multiplication of the Parts of a Speech................. 97
Epilogue 104
What Should Be Avoided by One Desirous of Brevity as Well as
by One Desirous of Copia 105
Peroration 106

INDEX OF FIGURES
English and Latin

Abominatio 37
Abusio 30
Acclamatio 82
Accumulatio 59
Admiratio 37
Aequipollentia 33
Allegory 30
Amplification 35
Antonomasia 27
Apologue 84
Apostrophe 26
Apothegms 80
Asseveration 102
Asyndeton 36
Auxesis 35
Catachresis 30
Circuitio 27
Collatio 30, 73, 78
Commemoratio 74
Comparatio 58, 73
Comparatives 34
Compositio 36
Constructio 37
Contentio 79
Contrarium 73, 83
Correctio 60
Delectatio 102
Deflexio 28
Demonstration 49

[109]

Digressio 55

Diminutio 35

Dissimile 73

Divisio 65

Dubitatio 37

Effictio 53

Egressio 55

Enallage 25

Epanalepsis 36

Epiphonema 82

Etymologia 27

Evidentia 47

Excursus 55

Exemplum 67

Expolitio 83

Fabula 67, 70

Fictio 63

Finitio 28

Homologia 24

Hyperbole 35

Imagio 78

Incrementum 58

Induction 78

Intellectio 33

Interpretatio 24

Iteratio 25

Judicia 80

Metalepsis 31

Metaphor 28

Metonymy 32

Noema 82

Notatio 28, 51

Onomatopoeia 31

Parable 73

Paragoge 31

Periphrasis 27

Polysyndeton 36

Propositions 60

Prosopographia 51

Prosopopoeia 50

Ratiocinatio 59

Relatives 34

Sententia 80

Sermocinatio 53, 98
Sermones 86
Simile 73
Similitudio 30, 73
Synecdoche 33
Synonomia L.. 19
Subjectio 37
Superlatio 35
Topographia 54
Topothesia 54
Translatio 28
Transumptio 31
Zeugma 36

Greek

'Ακόλουθα 29
'Ανακόλουθα 29
'Αποδέιξις... 49
Δείνωσις... 24
Διαλογιομός 53
Εἰκών 78
'Ενέργεια.. 47
'Επαγωγή... 78
'Επιδιήγησις... 99
'Επιφώνημα... 82
'Ετέρωσις.. 25
'Ισοδυναμία.. 33
Κρίσεις.. 80
Μείωσις 35
'Ομοίωσις 73
Παράδειγμα 67
Παρέκβασις... 55
Περιοτάσεις 57
Πίστεις.. 66
Συναθροισμός... 24, 59
Σύνταξις... 37
Τοπογραφία... 54
'Υποτυπώσις.. 49
Χρεία.. 56
Χρονογραφία.. 55